Software Faults Diagnosis in Complex Mission Critical Systems

Gabriella Carrozza

Software Faults Diagnosis in Complex Mission Critical Systems

A novel, recovery oriented, approach

LAP LAMBERT Academic Publishing

Impressum / Imprint
Bibliografische Information der Deutschen Nationalbibliothek: Die Deutsche Nationalbibliothek verzeichnet diese Publikation in der Deutschen Nationalbibliografie; detaillierte bibliografische Daten sind im Internet über http://dnb.d-nb.de abrufbar.
Alle in diesem Buch genannten Marken und Produktnamen unterliegen warenzeichen-, marken- oder patentrechtlichem Schutz bzw. sind Warenzeichen oder eingetragene Warenzeichen der jeweiligen Inhaber. Die Wiedergabe von Marken, Produktnamen, Gebrauchsnamen, Handelsnamen, Warenbezeichnungen u.s.w. in diesem Werk berechtigt auch ohne besondere Kennzeichnung nicht zu der Annahme, dass solche Namen im Sinne der Warenzeichen- und Markenschutzgesetzgebung als frei zu betrachten wären und daher von jedermann benutzt werden dürften.

Bibliographic information published by the Deutsche Nationalbibliothek: The Deutsche Nationalbibliothek lists this publication in the Deutsche Nationalbibliografie; detailed bibliographic data are available in the Internet at http://dnb.d-nb.de.
Any brand names and product names mentioned in this book are subject to trademark, brand or patent protection and are trademarks or registered trademarks of their respective holders. The use of brand names, product names, common names, trade names, product descriptions etc. even without a particular marking in this work is in no way to be construed to mean that such names may be regarded as unrestricted in respect of trademark and brand protection legislation and could thus be used by anyone.

Coverbild / Cover image: www.ingimage.com

Verlag / Publisher:
LAP LAMBERT Academic Publishing
ist ein Imprint der / is a trademark of
OmniScriptum GmbH & Co. KG
Heinrich-Böcking-Str. 6-8, 66121 Saarbrücken, Deutschland / Germany
Email: info@lap-publishing.com

Herstellung: siehe letzte Seite /
Printed at: see last page
ISBN: 978-3-659-67232-3

Zugl. / Approved by: UNIVERSITY OF NAPLES FEDERICO II, Dissertation 2008

Table of Contents

iv

List of Tables

List of Figures

Table of Contents

List of Tables

List of Figures

Introduction

Hardware and software technologies are progressing fast, dramatically increasing the complexity of modern computer systems. Large scale and distributed infrastructures are being increasingly employed, even in the context of critical scenarios; programs are being developed according to modular software architectures, typically based on Off-The-Shelf (OTS) software items. These allow industries to be competitive by reducing the development costs and the time to market.

Over the last decade, computers are enabling crucial human everyday activities, such as public economy, large scale critical infrastructures management (e.g., for water and power supply plants and energy production), and air traffic control. Given the growing dependence on computers in these life- and cost-critical applications, dependability becomes an essential demand: a failure, indeed, can be catastrophic in terms of business or, even worse, human losses.

Business critical systems, e.g., for e-commerce or e-government applications, have to maximize system availability and service reliability in order to maximize customers' satisfaction and survive today's competition. Since these systems are widely distributed to users with different and unknown usage patterns, developing dependability strategies becomes quite complicated. This holds also for everyday critical systems, e.g., hospitals or banks, which rely on databases management systems whose failures would deeply affect individuals or groups. Conversely, mission and safety critical systems have a narrow set of target users, and usage patterns are predictable in many cases. For these systems, the dependability level is regulated by standard specifications, carried out by international bodies, to which commercial products have to be compliant (e.g., the DO-178B standard for avionics software certification [1]).

For these reasons, a great research effort is being devoted to the dependability evaluation, assessment and improvement of complex software. In particular, testing and verification activities, along with fault tolerance techniques are massively used to satisfy dependability requirements.

The key **for achieving fault tolerance is the ability to accurately detect, diagnose, and recover from faults during system operation**. The great research effort striven in fault tolerant systems has provided good results with respect to hardware-related errors and faults. In most of the cases, these are easy to reproduce and repair, e.g., stuck-at or bit flips. Recent and eminent references addressing these issues are [2], [3], [4].

Conversely, software faults, which have been demonstrated to be the major cause of systems [5], [6], are neither easy to characterize nor to recover, hence they represent the major matter of concern for complex systems dependability.

---

[1]http://www.lynuxworks.com/solutions/milaero/do-178b.php3

A plenty of studies, from the dependability and software engineering communities, demonstrated that **the manifestation of a software fault, i.e., a software error, can be permanent as well as transient**. According to this, software faults have been classified in *Bohrbugs*, which result in permanent errors, and *Heisenbugs* which instead manifest transiently. While the former can be discovered successfully by means of traditional testing and static analysis techniques, the latter elude the testing process and cannot be reproduced systematically [7]. Studies on field data analysis showed that most of software faults fall within *Heisenbugs*, in that they are due to overloads, timing and exception errors or race conditions, i.e., to environmental factors which can vary over time [8, 9]. The problem is exacerbated by the presence of OTS components whose well-known dependability pitfalls do not hold industries back from their usage in critical systems. In fact, their dependability behavior is unknown or difficult to characterize in that they can behave unpredictably when used out of the so-called *intended profile*, and when integrated with other components. Faults propagation is indeed exacerbated by integration: a fault can propagate in several ways and among several components, thus complicating the task of fault location. However, the identification of a fault could not suffice for dependability improvement: the bug could not be fixed due to the closed source nature of many OTS items. This results in the lack of an exhaustive failure modes characterization of the overall system at design/development time, thus making traditional dependability means (e.g., fault prevention, fault tolerance or fault removal during development) unsuitable for dealing with software faults. **Diagnosis seems to be a promising alternative to traditional means**, mainly for what fault location may concern. Several vocabulary definitions answer the question of what is diagnosis. From the ancient Greek $\delta\iota\alpha\gamma\iota\gamma\omega\sigma\kappa\epsilon\iota\nu$, which stands for *to discern*, *to distinguish*, they share the general meaning of identifying the nature and cause of some phenomenon. In the field of dependable systems, diagnosis aims to identify the root cause of a failure, i.e., the fault, starting from its outward symptoms.Existing diagnosis approaches, which mainly cope with hardware-induced errors and their symptoms within a software system, have to be revised in order to deal with software faults and their transient manifestations. With respect to hardware faults, these have to be discriminated in that they could induce unnecessary and costly recovery actions thus reducing available resources and affecting the reliability level of the overall system [2]. Software faults, instead, have to be properly taken into account since they could be catastrophic, and ad-hoc recovery actions have to be initiated when they occur. However, the problem of recovery costs still holds andit has to be faced by defining ad-hoc and fine grained recovery strategies.

Hence, a novel and recovery-oriented approach is needed in charge of diagnosing software faults and of coping with their transient manifestations.

Several challenges have to be faced when designing this approach. First, the presence of software faults hampers the definition of a simple, and accurate, mathematical model able to describe systems failure modes (hence, pure model based techniques become inadequate). Second, due to the presence of OTS components, low intrusiveness in terms of source code modifications is desirable. Third, diagnosis has to be performed on-line and automatically, i.e., a fault has to be located as soon as possible during system execution and with lack of human guidance. The reason for this is twofold. On the one hand, it is to fulfill strict time requirements, for system recovery and reconfiguration, in the case of a fault. On the other hand, it is to face system complexity with respect to ordinary system management and maintainance operations, whose manual execution would result in strenuous human efforts and long completion times.

Thesis Contributions

The efforts striven in this dissertation result into the design and implementation of a novel, holistic, approach for on-line Software Faults Diagnosis in complex and OTS based critical systems.

Detection (D), Location (L) and Recovery (R) have been integrated into the diagnosis process, leading to the design of a complex DLR framework. An integrated approach has not been proposed so far to perform diagnosis of software faults in complex and OTS based systems.

The intuition of combining fault detection and location has been desribed in some works addressing system level diagnosis [10, 11] to face the problem of transient manifestations, i.e., to manage the partial knowledge about the failure modes of the target system.

As for recovery, two points are worth noting. First, combining recovery actions with diagnosis allows the system to diagnose and recover from faults that would not be discoverable by using system diagnosis only, as stated in [12, 13]. Second, a recovery oriented approach is the key for achieving fault tolerance in that it allows to trigger actions which are tailored for the particular fault that occurred. The strong advantage of the proposed approach is that information related to the nature of the occurred faults are also provided when recovery is performed, which are useful (i) for alerting human operators if the fault is unknown and cannot be located and (ii) for off-line periodic maintainance of the target system.

The driving idea behind the overall approach is based on the machine learning paradigm, and dependencies exist among the three phases, which hold in the form of feedback actions. These are mainly aimed to improve detection quality over time, by reducing the number of false positives, and can be performed both manually or automatically. However, the whole process of diagnosis is designed to be performed on-line, i.e., to diagnose faults and to recover the system during its operational phase, differently from most of the previous work which proposed off-line/ on-site diagnosis approaches aiming to locate bugs in the source code, and sometimes the environmental conditions.

The most important contributions of this thesis, which bring an added value to the existing literature, are:

- The integration of detection, location and recovery into an integrated diagnosis process;

- The exploitation of OS support to detect application failures, as well as to support error detection in a location oriented perspective;

- The design of a location strategy in charge of managing unknown faults, i.e., the root causes of *field failures* which can manifest during system operational life;

- The application of the anomaly detection techniques to software faults diagnosis.

The DLR framework has been actually implemented in the form of a complex diagnosis engine, designed to work under the Linux environment. Its effectiveness has been evaluated on a real world case study, in the field of Air Traffic Control. Experiments show that the engine has been able to locate known faults at a good quality and low overhead. Good results have also been achieved in terms of the location of unknown faults, as well as of the reduction of false positives over time which was one of the most important requirements of the proposed detection strategy.

Thesis organization

A thorough analysis of existing literature, corroborated by the experiments conducted in this thesis, has highlighted the need for the DLR framework, i.e., of a holistic approach in charge of combining detection, location and recovery into an integrated process. In particular, this originates from the studies which have been conducted in this thesis focusing (i) on the detection and its impact on diagnosis and (ii) the importance of a recovery oriented approach for achieving fault tolerance in complex OTS based systems. In order to emphasize the role that each phase plays in the context of the DLR framework, the thesis has been organized following a top-down approach. It gives an overview of the overall framework, and of the proposed approach as well, in chapter 2, where the need for such a holistic view is justified by analyzing the related work. The following chapters have been devoted to discuss each phase of the DLR framework. Chapter 3 focuses on detection, whereas location and recovery are discussed in chapter 4. As the thesis is mainly based on experiments, aiming to corroborate theoretical intuitions or to demonstrate the effectiveness of proposed solutions, their discussion is spread all over the work. Experimental results related to the detection of kernel hangs and application failures are reported in chapter 3; DLR effectiveness is proved instead in chapter 5, where also a deep description of the case study is provided. To summarize, the reminder of the thesis has been organized as follows:

- Chapter 1 provides the basic concepts of dependability and of software dependability as well. Software faults, and the failure process are described thoroughly, emphasizing the problem of transient manifestations. The final part of the chapter is devoted to fault injection and to the related literature focusing on it.

- Chapter 2 describes the DLR framework and it gives an overview of the proposed approach. Its final part is devoted to the discussion of related work on fault diagnosis.

- Chapter 3 focuses of the problem of detection. It illustrates all the experimental studies which have been conducted in aiming to demonstrate the importance of the operating system support, as well as the impact of detection on the overall diagnosis quality.

- Chapter 4 describes the location phase, and the recovery actions as well. A description of the machine learning paradigm, and of the adopted classifiers is provided as well, in order to facilitate the comprehension for readers which are not skilled in this field.

- Chapter 5 is finally devoted to describe the case study and the experimental campaigns, as well as to discuss the achieved results.

If you trust before you try, you may
repent before you die.

Nathan Bailey, 1721

Chapter 1

Software dependability

Dependability is a complex attribute whose definition changed several times in the last decade. Indeed, the increasing complexity of systems has caused dependability to become a major concern, encompassing several aspects, from safety to security. Focus is on software dependability into which current research efforts are striven to face the problem of transient manifestation of software faults. In the first part of the chapter, fundamentals of dependability are provided. Then the focus moves to software dependability, devoting particular attention to the classification of software faults and the ways they can manifest. Last sections are devoted to fault injection, as it is currenty the most effective mean for dependability evaluation and assessment of complex software systems.

1.1 Software Dependability

Software is *design*, differently from any other engineering product. Its unreliability is only due to design faults, i.e., to the consequences of human failures. Hardware reliability, instead, is dominated by random physical factors affecting the components on which there is engineering knowledge enough to prevent failures. This is demonstrated by the several reliability theories

10

that have been developed so far for the realization of highly dependable hardware systems, as well as for hardware reliability evaluation and assessment.

Software is replacing older technologies in safety and mission critical applications (e.g., air traffic engine control, raiload interlocking, nuclear plants management), and it is moving from an auxiliary to a primary role in providing critical services (e.g., modern air traffic systems are being designed to handle much more traffic than in the past few years). Additionally, it is being used to solve novel problems, i.e., problems for which there is a lack of evidence from past history, as well as to perform difficult tasks which would be not possible otherwise (e.g., enhanced support to pilots in unstable aircrafts). If on the one hand this provides great advantages and reduces human efforts, on the other hand the more difficult the task, the greater the probability of mistakes which can even result in catastrophes, e.g.;

- *July 28, 1962 - Mariner I space probe.* A bug in the flight control software causes the Mariner I rocket to calculate the incorrect trajectory. The rocket was destroyed by Mission Control over the Atlantic.

- *1982 - Soviet gas pipeline.* A bug in the Soviet gas pipeline software controls caused the largest non-nuclear, man-made explosion in history.

- *1985-1987- Therac-25 medical accelerator.* A therapeutic device that utilizes radiation has a bug which can lead to a race condition. If that condition occurs then the patient receives multiple times the recommend dosage of radiation. The failure directly caused the deaths of five patients and harmed many more.

- *January 15, 1990 - AT&T Network Outage.* A bug in a new release of code causes the switches of AT&T to crash. Over 60 thousand New Yorkers were left without phone service for nine hours.

- *November 2000 – National Cancer Institute, Panama City.* The software of a therapeutic device that utilizes radiation for treatment delivers twice the recommended dosage. Eight patients die and 20 more will undoubtedly be permanently disabled.

- *May 2004 Mercedes-Benz - "Sensotronic" braking system* - Mercedes-Benz has to recall 680,000 cars due to a failure of its Sensotronic breaking system.

1.2   Basic Concepts of Dependability

Even if the effort on the definition of the basic concepts and terminology for computer systems dependability dates back to 1980, the milestone paper in the field of dependable systems is [14], which was published in 1985. Here dependability was defined as *the quality of the delivered service such that reliance can justifiably be placed on this service*, but the notion has evolved over the years. Recent efforts from the same community define the dependability as *the ability to avoid service failures that are more frequent and more severe than is acceptable* [15]. This last definition has been introduced since it does not stress the need for justification of reliance. The dependability is a composed quality attribute, that encompasses the following sub-attributes:

- **Availability**: readiness for correct service;

- **Reliability**: continuity of correct service;

- **Safety**: absence of catastrophic consequences on the user(s) and the environment;

- **Confidentiality**: absence of improper system alterations;

- **Maintainability**: ability to undergo modifications and repairs.

1.2.1 Threats

The causes that lead a system to deliver an incorrect service, i.e., a service deviating from its function, are manifold and can manifest at any phase of its life-cycle. Hardware faults and design errors are just an example of the possible sources of failure. These causes, along with the manifestation of incorrect service, are recognized in the literature as dependability threats, and are commonly categorized as *failures, errors,* and *faults* [15].

A **failure** is an event that occurs when the delivered service deviates from correct service. A service fails either because it does not comply with the functional specification, or because this specification did not adequately describe the system function. A service failure is a transition from correct service to incorrect service, i.e., to not implementing the system function. The period of delivery of incorrect service is a service outage. The transition from incorrect service to correct service is a service recovery or repair. The deviation from correct service may assume different forms that are called *service failure modes* and are ranked according to *failure severities.*

An **error** can be regarded as the part of a system's total state that may lead to a failure. In other words, a failure occurs when the error causes the delivered service to deviate from the correct service. The adjudged or hypothesized cause of an error is called a **fault**. Faults can be either internal or external of a system, and they can be classified in several ways (e.g., basing on their nature, or the way they manifest in errors).

Failures, errors, and faults are related each other in the form of a *chain of threats* [15], as sketched in figure 1.1. A fault is *active* when it produces an error; otherwise, it is *dormant.* An active fault is either i) an internal fault that was previously dormant and that has been activated, or ii) an external fault. A failure occurs when an error is *propagated* to the service interface and causes the service delivered by the system to deviate from correct service. An

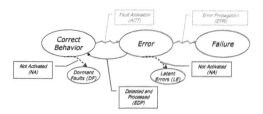

Figure 1.1: The propagation chain: fault, error, failure

error which does not lead the system to failure is said to be a *latent* error. A failure of a system component *causes* an internal fault of the system that contains such a component, or causes an external fault for the other system(s) that receive service from the given system.

The dependability attributes can be formalized mathematically, and basic measures have been introduced in charge of quantifying them.

The reliability, $R(t)$, was the only dependability measure of interest to early designers of dependable computer systems. It is the the conditional probability of delivering a correct service in the interval $[0, t]$, given that the service was correct at the reference time 0 [16]:

$$R(0, t) = P(no\ failures\ in\ [0, t] | correct\ service\ in\ 0) \tag{1.1}$$

Let us call $F(t)$ the unreliability function, i.e., the cumulative distribution function of the failure time. The reliability function can thus be written as:

$$R(t) = 1 - F(t) \tag{1.2}$$

Since reliability is a function of the mission duration T, mean time to failure (MTTF) is often used as a single numeric indicator of system reliability [17]. In particular, the time to failure (TTF) of a system is defined as the interval of time between a system recovery and the consecutive failure.

As for availability, they say a system to be available at a the time t if it is able to provide a correct service at that instant of time. The availability can thus be thought as the expected value $E(A(t))$ of the following $A(t)$ function:

$$A(t) = \begin{cases} 1 & if \ proper \ service \ at \ t \\ 0 & otherwise \end{cases} \tag{1.3}$$

In other terms, the availability is the fraction of time that the system is operational. The measuring of the availability became important with the advent of time-sharing systems. These systems brought with it an issue for the continuity of computer service and thus minimizing the "down time" became a prime concern. Availability is a function not only of how rarely a system fails but also of how soon it can be repaired upon failure. Clearly, a synthetic availability indicator can be computed as:

$$Av = \frac{MTTF}{MTTF + MTTR} = \frac{MTTF}{MTBF} \tag{1.4}$$

where MTBF = MTTF + MTTR is the mean time between failures. The time between failures (TBF) is the time interval between two consecutive failures. Obviously, this measure makes sense only for the so-called repairable systems.

$R(t)$ and $A(t)$ are the dependability attributes of major interest for this dissertation. A complete dissertation about dependability fundamentals can be found in [15], along with a description of dependability measures.

1.2.2 Means

Dependability means can be grouped into four major categories [15]:

- **Fault prevention**, to prevent the occurrence or introduction of faults. It is enforced during the design phase of a system, both for software (e.g., information hiding, modularization, use of strongly-typed programming languages) and hardware (e.g., design rules).

- **Fault tolerance**, to avoid service failures in the presence of faults. It takes place during the operational life of the system. A widely used method of achieving fault tolerance is redundancy, either temporal or spatial. Temporal redundancy attempts to reestablish proper operation by bringing the system in a error-free state and by repeating the operation which caused the failure, while spatial redundancy exploits the computation performed by multiple system's replicas. The former is adequate for transient faults, whereas the latter can be effective only under the assumption that the replicas are not affected by the same permanent faults. This can be achieved through design diversity [18]. Both temporal and spatial redundancy requires error detection and recovery techniques to be in place: upon error detection (i.e., the ability to identify that an error occurred in the system), a recovery action is performed.
  The measure of effectiveness of any given fault tolerance technique is called its coverage, i.e, the percentage of the total number of failures that are successfully recovered by the fault tolerance mean.

- **Fault removal**, to reduce the number and severity of faults. The removal activity is usually performed during the verification and validation phases of the system development, by means of testing and/or fault injection [19]. However, fault removal can also be done during the operational phase, in terms of corrective and perfective maintenance.

- **Fault forecasting**, to estimate the present number, the future incidence, and the likely consequences of faults. Fault forecasting is conducted by evaluating the system behavior with respect to fault occurrence or activation. Evaluation cna be (i) qualitative, aiming at identifying, classifying, and ranking the failure modes that would lead to system failures and (ii), quantitative evaluation, aiming at evaluating the extent to which some of the attributes are satisfied in terms of probabilities; those attributes are then viewed as measures. The quantitative evaluation can be performed at different phases of the system's life cycle: the design phase, the prototype phase and the operational phase [20]. In the design phase, the dependability can be evaluated via modeling and simulation, including simulated fault injection. During the operational phase, field failure data analysis (FFDA) can be performed, aiming at measuring the dependability attributes of a system according to the failures that naturally manifest during system operation. When using FFDA, several issues arise related to data collection, filtering and analysis, which are extensively addressed in [20].

1.2.3   Software faults

The cause of a software error is always a bug, i.e., a software defect, which is permanent since it lies into the code. This means that, if a program contains a bug, any circumstances that cause it to fail once will always cause it to fail. This is the reason for which software failures are often referred to as "systematic failures" [21]. However, the *failure process*, i.e., the way bugs are activated does not follow such a deterministic behavior at all. During the execution of a program, the sequence of inputs, as well as the execution environment, cannot be predicted, hence it is not possible to know with certainty which are the program's faults, and then its failures.Environmental conditions can activate a given fault rather than another one, within a given execution of the program. This is especially true with respect to complex and concurrent applications, in which sources of non determinism hold, due to multithreading for example. Hence, it is licit to say that software faults can manifest transiently. However, there are also faults which manifest permanently. These are likely to be fixed and discovered during the pre-operational phases of the system life cycle (e.g., structured design, design review, quality assurance, unit, component and integration testing, alpha/beta test).

Software faults have been recognized to be the major cause of systems outages by J.Gray in 1986 [5]. Since there, several attempts have been made to give a systematic view of the kinds of faults which can affect a program. The first one, which is still a fundamental milestone in the field of software dependability, is the Orthogonal Defect Classification (ODC) of software faults, dating back to 1992 [22]. Its main contribution lies in the definition of a scientific approach suitable for a large class of systems, differently from the bespoke solutions which were used before then. Indeed, it provides usable measurements that give insights into the quality of the development process. Before ODC, evaluating a process, diagnosing a problem, benchmarking, or assessing the effectiveness of testing were tasks that could not be executed with scientific rigor.

1.2.4 Orthogonal Defect Classification

ODC encompasses software defects and triggers. The former are the "bugs", whereas the latter encompass those conditions which potentially activate faults thus letting them surface. Software defects are grouped into orthogonal, non overlapping, defect types. Hence, a defect type and one or more triggers are associated to each defect, as sketched in Figure 1.2.

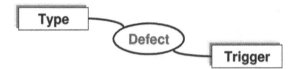

Figure 1.2: Key concepts of ODC classification

The following defect types are encompassed in [22]:

- Function - The fault affects significant capability, end-user interfaces, interface with hardware architecture or global data structures and should require a formal design change. Usually these faults affect a considerable amount of code and refer to capabilities either implemented incorrectly or not implemented at all.

- Interface - This defect type corresponds to errors in interacting with other components, modules or device drivers, via macros, call statements, control blocks or parameters lists.

- Assignment - The fault involves a few lines of code, such as the initialization of control blocks or data structures. The assignment may be either missing or wrongly implemented.

- Checking - This defect addresses program logic that has failed to properly validate data and values before they are used. Examples are missing or incorrect validation of parameters or data in conditional statements.

- Timing/Serialization - Missing or incorrect necessary serialization of shared resources, wrong resources serialized or wrong serialization technique employed. Examples are deadlocks or missed deadline in hard real time systems.

- Algorithm - This defect include efficiency and correctness problems that affect the task and can be fixed by (re)implementing an algorithm or local data structure without the need for requesting a design change.

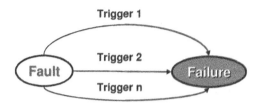

Figure 1.3: ODC triggers.

- Build/package/merge - Describe errors that occur due to mistakes in library systems, management of changes, or version control. Rather than being related to the product under development, this defect type is mainly related to the development process, since it affect tools used for software development such as code versioning systems.

- Documentation - This defect type affects both publication and maintenance notes. It has a significant meaning only in the early stages of software life cycle (Specification and High Level Design)

The concept of the software trigger was introduced in [8] where it was applied to failure analysis from defects in the MVS operating system, with the intention of guiding fault-injection. In the ODC perspective, they are defined as "catalysts" able to activate dormant software faults which surface as failures (see Figure 1.3). In an abstract sense, these are operators on the set of faults to map them into failures; in practice, they are broad environmental conditions or system activities. Faults which surface as failures for the first time after a product is released often have been dormant throughout the period of development, i.e., they have not been discovered even if extensive testing has been performed. Ideally, the defect trigger distribution exhibited on the field should be similar to the distribution observed in the test environment: significant discrepancies between the two highlihgt potential problems in the system test environment. There are specific requirements for a set of triggers to be considered part of ODC. Basically, it requires that the distribution of an attribute (such as trigger) changes as a function of the activity (process phase or time), to characterize the process. The most used defect trigger categories are:

- Boundary Conditions - Software defects were triggered when the systems ran in particularly critical conditions (e.g.: low memory).

- Bug Fix - The defect surfaced after another defect was corrected. This may happen either because the bug fixed allowed users to executed a previously untested (and buggy) area of the system, because in the same component where the bug was fixed there was another undiscovered bug, or because the fix was not successfully, in that it caused another defects on the same (or on a different) component.

- Recovery - The defect surfaced after the system recovered from a previous failure.

- Exception Handling - The defect surfaced after an unforeseen exception handling path was triggered.

- Timing - The defect emerged when particular timing conditions were met (e.g.: the application was deployed on a system with a different thread scheduler).

- Workload - The defect surfaced only when particular workload condition were met (e.g.: only after the number of concurrent requests to serve was higher than a particular threshold).

While defects give information about the development process, triggers are in charge of providing feedback about the verification process. Triggers and defect-type can be used in conjunction: the cross-product of defect type and trigger provides information that can estimate the effectiveness of the process.

ODC addresses the problem of providing feedback to developers, which is a key issue of measurement in the software development process. Without feedback to the development team, the value of measurement is questionable and defeats the very purpose of data collection. It fills the gap between statistical testing and causal analysis of defects, which is due to the lack of fundamental cause-effect relationship extractable from the process. Its semantic power and orthogonality between products, have let ODC to be the starting point for achieving many others research goal.

Beyond ODC

In [1], ODC has been extended for faults emulation and injection purposes. In authors' opinion, the fault types provided by ODC are too broad for practical injection purposes, hence they propose a further refinement of ODC fault classes by analyzing faults from the point of view of the (program) context in which they occur, and by relating the faults with programming language constructs. From this perspective, a defect is one or more programming language construct that is either missing, wrong, or in excess. Hence, they classified each fault according to its nature: *missing, wrong* or *extraneous* construct. In particular, the classification has been performed by following three steps, starting by data collected on the field from several widely used software tools (e.g., CDEX data extractor or MingW). ODC has been used as a first step. In the second step, faults were grouped according to the nature of the defect, defined from a building block programming perspective. For each ODC class a software fault is characterized by one programming language constructs that may be either missing, wrong or superfluous (instead, in ODC, the cause of software defect can be an incorrect or a missing construct). In the third and last step, faults were further refined and classified in specific types. The final result is the identification of 18 fault types, covering all the ODC faults categories, as shown in Table 1.1.

Table 1.1: Extended ODC classification by Madeira et al. [1]

Fault nature	Fault specific types	# Faults	ASG	CHK	INT	ALG	FUN
Missing	*if* construct plus statements (MIFS)	71				✓	
	AND sub-*expr* in expression used as branch condition (MLAC)	47	✓				
	function call (MFC)	46				✓	
	if construct around statements (MIA)	34	✓				
	OR sub-*expr* in expression used as branch condition (MLOC)	32	✓				
	small and localized part of the algorithm (MLPA)	23				✓	
	variable assignment using an expression (MVAE)	21	✓				
	functionality (MFCT)	21					✓
	variable assignment using a value (MVAV)	20	✓				
	if construct plus statements plus *else* before statements (MIEB)	18				✓	
	variable initialization (MVIV)	15	✓				
Wrong	logical expression used as branch condition (WLEC)	22		✓			
	algorithm - large modifications (WALL)	20					✓
	value assigned to variable (WVAV)	16	✓				
	arithmetic expression in parameter of function call (WAEP)	14			✓		
	data types or conversion used (WSUT)	12	✓				
	variable used in parameter of function call (WPFV)	11			✓		
Extraneous	variable assignment using another variable (EVAV)	9	✓				

1.2.5 The failure process

The idea of triggers as catalysts for software faults surfacing, comes from the Gray's intuition that *software faults are soft*, similarly to some hardware, transient, faults [5]. The author conjectured that some faults exist for which "if the program state is reinitialized and the failed operation retried, the operation will usually not fail the second time".

With respect to ODC, this can be related to the concept of "field faults", i.e., residual faults which escaped pre-operational quality assessment activities (e.g., testing campaigns), and which did not surface even for months or years of production. These faults are due to strange hardware conditions (rare or transient device fault), limit conditions (out of storage, counter overflow, lost interrupt, etc.) or race conditions (forgetting to request a semaphore). The trickiest issue when dealing with them is reproducibility: activation conditions depend on complex

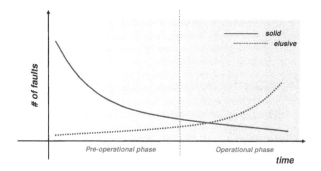

Figure 1.4: Evolution of software faults during system life

combinations of the internal state and the external environment (i.e.: the set made by up other programs, services, libraries, virtual machines, middleware and operating systems the applications interacts with). Hence, they occur rarely and can be very difficult to reproduce: this dramatically complicates the tasks of error detection and faults diagnosis. As such a behavior recall Heisenberg Uncertainty Principle in Physics, these faults are well known as *"Heisenbugs"* or elusive faults. Conversely, software faults which are easily reproducible (e.g., through a debugger) are called solid faults or *"Bohrbugs"*. These are likely to disappear over time, differently from Heisenbugs which rather increase with time, as shown in Figure 1.4. This is because solid bugs are almost completely removed during the pre-release phases of the software, by means debugging of and testing, as well as of structured design. In a recent work by Trivedi, a further class of software faults has been defined: *Mandelbugs* [23]. They are faults whose activation is just apparently nondeterministic: actually, there exists a condition under which the fault is deterministically activated, but detecting this condition is so difficult that the bug is labeled as non-deterministic. This usually happens with complex software systems employing one or more interacting OTS items. Mandelbugs are easily misinterpreted as Heisenbugs. However they are different in practice: the former are bugs whose causes are so complex that its behavior appears chaotic, whereas the latter are computer bugs that disappear or alter its characteristics.

1.2.6   Fault Injection for Software Dependability evaluation

Fault injection is the deliberate insertion of faults or errors (upsets) into a computer system in order to determine its response [24]. It has been widely and effectively used for (i) measuring the parameters of analytical dependability models [25](ii), validating existing fault-tolerant systems [26] (iii), observing how systems behave in the presence of faults [19], and for comparing different systems[27].

It was first employed in the 1970s, and for the first decade it has been used exclusively by the industry for measuring the coverage and latency parameters of highly reliable systems. Academia approached fault injection not until the mid-1980s, when initial work concentrated on understanding error propagation and analyzing the efficiency of new fault-detection mechanisms. Since there, research has expanded to include characterization of dependability at the system level and its relationship to the workload. However, in both the academic community and industry, the most of the efforts have been devoted to study the effects of physical hardware faults, i.e. faults caused by wear-out or external disturbances. Since they have been recognized as the major cause of systems failure [5], research is changing its directions, paying a greater attention to the injection of software faults. So far, studies concerning with software faults are few, especially when compared to the plethora of works addressing hardware reliability and its assessment via fault injection.

The transition from hardware to software faults injection is being painful for researchers in this field. The main why is the limited knowledge which is available about software faults, along with the difficulties rising from their scarce reproducibility. However, the wide know how which

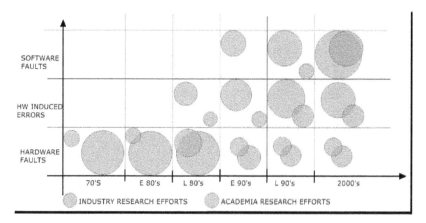

Figure 1.5: Efforts striven into fault injection by both industry and academia since the last decades. Overlapping circles indicates the extent of the cooperation

has been built for decades on hardware faults injection and dependability evaluation has been partially leveraged from researchers in the field of software dependability, e.g., by adapting hardware injection techniques to the injection of software faults.

Figure 1.5 shows the evolution of research about fault injection since 70's. It confirms that these days software faults are the major concern for both industry and academia.

Since the focus of this dissertation is on software faults, and on how to detect and locate them within a complex system, the attention is devoted to software faults injection. As stated in [28], it acts as a "cristal ball" in that it is able to provide worst-case predictions about how badly a piece of code might behave, differently from testing which is rather able to assess *how good software is*.

1.2.7 Software Fault injection fundamentals

By software fault it is meant a software defect which in fact corresponds to a bug into the code. An error occurs if the fault is activated. It represents an erroneous state of the system (e.g., a wrong value into a memory register) which can lead to a failure if it propagates to the system interfaces, following the traditional definition of the propagation chain provided in [15] (see Figure1.1 in the previous section). Note that, the definition of software fault as a defect (i.e., the one used for ODC [8] implies that software requirements and specifications are assumed to be correct, even if this does not always hold in practice. However, these faults fall beyond the scope of this dissertation.

1.2.8 The WWW dilemma

While hardware faults are easy to inject since internal states can be eventually reduced to a couple of values ("0" or "1"), software internal states are not so simple, thus making researchers be in the horns of a great dilemma.

Even in a medium complex software program, many injection points exist and several injection points could be identified: **Where to inject**? Additionally, it has to be established the time for injecting the fault, as well as the time for its activation: **When to inject?**. Of course, much time can be spent conducting a fault injection experiment if the injected faults are rarely activated, hence the main question become: **What to inject?**. The **W.W.W. dilemma** has to be faced, whose major concern is the need for *representativeness*, i.e., injected faults should be representative of faults which can actually affect the target software in order to achieve meaningful results from the conducted experiments.

What to inject: injection or emulation? The most of the efforts have been striven so far in finding the most proper way to reproduce software faults via injection. Currently two main ways have been identified, which can be used to pursue different aims. Software faults can be reproduced either by modifying the source code of the target system i.e., by injecting the actual fault (Software Mutation, *SM*), or by means of error injection. *SM* consists of the injection of the most common programmer's mistakes into the source code. Such a pragmatic approach allows to exactly reproduce the effects of a fault, as well as of injected all the kinds of faults, e.g., all the ones encompassed by ODC. However, if compared with error injection and other injection approaches, it is more difficult to implement. First of all, it requires the availability of the source code hence it not suitable for closed source components, as well as for legacy systems which can be difficult to instrument. Additionally, as discussed in [29], it is not easy to guarantee that the injected faults actually correspond to the kinds of software faults that are most likely to be hidden in the code, and their probability of future manifestation. For these reason, *SM* results cannot be used as an absolute measure of risk; rather they are an effective way for predicting worst case scenarios in terms of software risks [30]. Hence, *SM* is considered as a "best effort" approach for reproducing software faults. In [31], this approach is used to compare disk and memory resistance to operating systems crashes.

Reproducing software faults via emulation, i.e., by error injection, is very effective mean to accelerate typical residual faults, which are rarely activated. In fact, it allows to emulate activations at a higher rate and to achieve the desired speedup of the fault activation ratio [30].Errors can be injected both at memory level, i.e., by altering locations content, and at procedures level, i.e., by corrupting input parameters and/or return values. The most common technique for error injection is Software Implemented Fault Injection, *SWIFI*. It has been traditionally and successfully used for hardware faults emulation via software: since hardware functionality is largely visible through software, faults at various levels of the system can be emulated. Several tools have been implemented in charge of completely automating the process of injection, both of permanent and transient faults [32, 33, 34]. Recent studies have shown that many types of software faults can be emulated either by traditional *SWIFI* as well [35, 36]. In practice, the target software application is interrupted (e.g., by means of a trap), and specific fault injection routines that emulate faults by inserting errors in different parts of the system (processor registers, memory) are executed, prior to resume the correct run of the program. As for hardware faults, tools have also been implemented for injecting software faults (e.g., [32]). When dealing with software faults, the major drawback of *SWIFI* is that it does not allow to reproduce software faults which require large modifications to the code, or which are due to design deficiencies, i.e., Algorithm and Function Faults (see the classification in [8]), which account for a great part of software faults in complex systems [1].

SM and *SWIFI* have been experimentally compared in [29], which is a seminal work investigating the benefits and drawbacks of both the techniques in terms of (i) the cost of setup and execution time for using the techniques and (ii), the impact of the test case, fault type and error type on the failure symptoms of the target system. It demonstrates that injecting faults into the code, i.e., by means of *SM*, is definitely more accurate than *SWIFI*, in terms of faults representativeness. The cost related results, instead, are in favour of *SWIFI* which requires shorter setup and execution times.

A further alternative for emulating software faults is a binary mutation technique, named *G-SWFIT*, which has been proposed by Madeira et al. in [1]. Similarly to *SM*, it is a fault injection technique which corrupts executable code, rather than the source code. Hence, *SM* and *G-SWFIT* share the goal of emulating the most common high level programming mistakes, but they differ in the target system level. The latter injects faults by mutations introduced at the machine-code level. In practice, it consists of the emulation of high level software fault through the modification of the ready-to-run binary code of the target software module. The modifications are such that they introduce specific changes corresponding to the code that would have been generated by the compiler if the software faults were in the high-level source code. *G-SWFIT* is performed in two steps. First, the fault locations are identified before the actual experimentation, resulting in the set of faults to be injected. Then, the faults are actually injected during the target execution. As the fault locations have been previously identified, the task of injection is low intrusive. The main advantage of emulating the software faults at the machine-code level is that software faults can be injected even when the source code of the target application is not available: this is very important for the evaluation of OTS modules. Additionally, differently from other software fault injection techniques (e.g., corruption of parameters in API calls, or bit-flipping data and address spaces) it tries to emulate the existence of the fault itself and not to emulate its potential effects. This means that by using *G-SWFIT*, faults are injected which are due to actual software defects, thus achieving a better degree of authenticity of the system behavior. However, when using *G-SWFIT*, it is tricky to assure that injection locations actually reflect the high-level constructs where faults are prone to appear, and that binary mutations are the same as generated by source code mutations. Additionally, it requires a deep knowledge of the compiler generated instruction pattern, as well as of the optimization settings used by compilers.

Where to inject. Regardless of what you are injecting, errors or faults, the injection location is a crucial variable.

In the case of *SM*, faults can be injected both at components interfaces and internally, i.e., by modifying the internal source code of the target components. The main goal of injection at interfaces is to assess how sensitive the system is to faults in any of its software components, and to emulate possible faults propagations. Interface faults can be injected directly at the interface between components to simulate the situation where a component fails and outputs corrupted information to the other components. The basic assumption is that parameter corruptions at procedure calls reasonably emulate a real residual fault in the caller component. However, there is no guarantee that injected values really correspond to faults generated by the procedure invocation. Eminent studies injected faults at components interface, especially in the context of robustness testing. In [37] faults have been injected at Driver Programming Interface (DPI) to test the robustness of the Linux kernel; injection at System Call Interface (SCI) has rather been performed by means of Ballista injection tool[1].

Internal injection, instead, aims to uncover system pitfalls due to fault of its software modules. Internal hardware and software faults have been injected into the UNIX kernel by means of FINE, which is a tool in charge of injecting faults and monitoring the target system [38]. Authors mainly focus on hardware faults propagation within the system, and they propose a valuable methodology for internal injection, which can be applied to several contexts.

In [39] it has been demonstrated that these injection techniques are not equivalent, as they result in different system behaviors. In particular, by means of an experimental campaign, authors demonstrated that injection at component interfaces, which is generally simpler to implement than internal injection, does not represent residual software faults well. Furthermore, interface faults are not "representative" of internal faults as they do not have the same impact on system dependability, i.e., internal faults cannot be emulated through the injection of interface faults. However, both the two alternatives can be used together.

In the case of error injection, the problem of where to inject errors has been thoroughly faced in [35]. Authors state that the joint distribution of *faults over components* and *error types over faults*, i.e., the fault-error mapping, should be used to pinpoint injection locations. Once this joint distribution has been drawn, errors can be selected in a random way among all the available locations. Of course, that joint distribution is gathered by field data.

When to inject Once again, the problem of finding the right time for injection holds both for faults and error injection.

In the former case, when the source code of a given software component is modified, faults

---

[1]http://ltp.sourceforge.net

are activated each time the corrupted piece of code is executed. This means that a fault is present for the whole duration of an experiment. As for error injection, the problem is slightly more complicated in that it is not easy to establish when a fault is actually activated, i.e., it manifests as an error.

1.3 Related research on fault injection

Literature dealing with fault injection is abundant. It has been used to pursue several aims, from dependability benchmarking to fault tolerant systems validation. However, there is still a knowledge gap between injection of hardware and software faults. As for these, studies have been mainly focused on software development phase, resulting in an improvement of software development and testing methodologies, as well as of software reliability modeling and risk analysis. However, little has been done with respect to the operational phase of software systems, during which the operational environment and the software maturity cannot be neglected. During this phase, "field faults" (see [1]) can manifest which have never occurred during the pre-deployment phase, hence software reliability should be studied in the context of the whole system. This is especially true in the context of modular OTS systems in which integration is a source of unpredictable behavior. The main difficulties to be faced in this face come from (i) the need for collecting data (hence instrumentation is required in many cases) and, (ii) the impact of system architecture (hardware and software).

1.3.1 Fault tolerance validation of complex systems

Fault tolerance validation is the natural field of application of fault injection. Eminent works focus on this topic, since early 90s. A large number of studies have shown the efficiency of the fault tolerance algorithms and mechanisms on the dependability of a wide range of systems and architectures (e.g., [40]), hence the determination of the appropriate model for the fault tolerance process and proper estimation of the associated coverage parameters is essential. Fault injection is particularly attractive to this aim as it is able to test fault tolerance with respect to the faults that they are intended to tolerate, by speeding up the occurrence of errors and failures. As pointed out in [41], fault injection addresses both fault removal and fault forecasting. With respect to the fault removal objective, fault injection is explicitly aimed at reducing, by verification, the presence of design and implementation faults. As for fault forecasting, instead, the main issue is to rate, by evaluation, the efficiency of the operational behavior of the fault tolerance mechanisms and algorithms, e.g., their coverage. However, the fault tolerance coverage estimations obtained through fault injection experiments are estimates of conditional probabilistic measures characterizing dependability. They need to be related to the fault occurrence and activation rates to derive overall measures of system dependability. For what concerns software faults, the most common strategies for achieving fault tolerance are wrapping, N-version programming and diversity. The effectiveness of such techniques can be proved by fault injection, as it has been done in [42] by means of the MAFALDA injection tool.

1.3.2 Software Testing

Fault injection is widely used as a mean for conducting software testing campaigns, to the ultimate aim of testing the software in extreme and stressful conditions. In fact, injecting faults into the code is an effective way to quantify the impact of software faults from the user's point of view, and to get a quantitative idea of the potential risk represented by residual faults. This allows the optimization of the testing phase effort by performing risk assessment and prediction of worst-case scenarios. For example, if the injection of software faults in a given component causes a high percentage of catastrophic failures in the system, it means that residual software faults in that component may represent a high risk and more effort should be put into the testing. Additionally, fault injection allows to perform "what-if" analysis, which cannot be performed by traditional statistical testing techniques. Examples of fault injection campaigns in the context of software testing can be found in [43], where faults are injected via "assertion violation" to improve test coverage (e.g., to test recovery code which often remains untested even being error prone), and in [44] in which authors present a methodology for fault injection in distributed-memory parallel computers that use a message-passing paradigm. Their approach is based on injection of faults into interprocessor communications, and allows emulation of fault models commonly used in design of fault-tolerant parallel algorithms.

1.3.3 Robustness Testing

Robustness is defined as the degree to which a system operates correctly in the presence of exceptional inputs or stressful environmental conditions (see IEEE Std 610.12.1990). Robustness testing aims to develop test cases and test environments to assess the robustness of both OTS items before integrating them into an existing software system and of the robustness of a whole software system before moving it to the operational stage. Hence, it has not been designed to be performed on operational systems. **Fault injection is used to perform robustness testing, in the form of invalid/out of range input injection on the interfaces of the target application/API/system** (e.g.: an empty string on the file name parameter of an fopen() call).

A robustness test requires several steps. First system interfaces to test have been chosen, then both valid and invalid inputs are selected according to the expected behavior of the system (which can be retrieved from system specification or API reference manuals). The behavior of the system is then observed. The success criteria which is generally used with respect to robustness tests is "if it does not crash or hang, then it is robust", hence there is no need for an oracle. If a failure occurs, this failure is classified according to a failure severity scale. In [45], the 5-point **"CRASH"** scale has been defined for grading the severity of robustness vulnerabilities encountered, as well as for describing the result of robustness tests[2].

The first works on robustness testing date back to early 90's (e.g., [46]). However, the major efforts have been striven few years later, when [45] has been published comparing five UNIX based OSs, and when the desirable features of a benchmark for system robustness are defined in [47], along with a novel approach to build robustness benchmarks. The name of Ballista is tightly related to robustness testing. It is a suite allowing automated robustness testing by means of testing tools in charge of characterizing the exception handling effectiveness of software modules. For example, Ballista testing can find ways to make operating systems crash in response to exceptional parameters used for system calls, and can find ways to make other software packages suffer abnormal termination instead of gracefully returning error indications. It is a "black box" software testing tool, and is works well on testing the APIs of OTS (even Commercial, i.e., COTS) modules [48]. The suite has been first introduced in [49], dating back to 1998.

Robustness testing has been widely applied to OSs. Koopman at al. in [50] discuss the comparison between the robustness of different families of Operating Systems, namely Windows and Linux. The paper presents a novel approach to define benchmarks which are portable across OTS items with deeply different interfaces. Indeed, while previous work compared the robustness of Operating System with a similar System Call Interface (Unix-based OSes), in this work the robustness of several version of the Windows Operating System is compared to Linux's robustness, by identifying common groups of system calls and then analyzing the robustness for

---

[2]CRASH is the acronym for **C**atastrophic, **R**estart, **A**bort, **S**ilent, **H**indering.

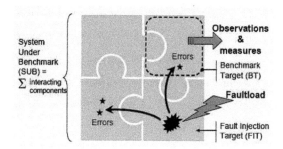

Figure 1.6: Dependability Benchmarking Components

each of these groups. [37] discusses the impact of faulty drivers on the robustness of the Linux kernel. By emulating faults at Driver Programming Interface Level (DPI), that implements the way device drivers interact with the kernel, this paper provides useful insights into the failure modes due to drivers' faults and into the degree of robustness of a target kernel with respect to faulty drivers. The information gathered also enables to improve these interaction facilities.

1.3.4 Dependability Benchmarking

Dependability benchmarking has been introduced in 1997 and it aims to assess and characterize the dependability level of a target system [47]. In particular, basing on fault injection, it allows to evaluate dependability features of a component or sub-system of the whole system, as well as to make comparative analysis between different systems.

A dependability benchmark is *"the specification of a standard procedure to assess dependability related measures of a computer system or computer component"* [27].

Figure 1.6, drawn from [27], depicts the most important components of a dependability benchmark. The **Benchmark Target (BT)** is the component or subsystem which is the target of the benchmark with respect to its application area and operating environment. Dependability measures (i.e.: the results of the dependability benchmark) are taken on the BT (by either direct on indirect measurement), hence it has not to be altered by the experiments (e.g., by injecting faults or by installing an invasive monitoring system).

The **System Under Benchmarking (SUB)** is the wider system which includes the above described BT. For instance the SUB may be an Operating System while the Benchmark Target may be a particular driver.

The **Workload** represents a typical operational profile applied to the SUB in order to benchmark the dependability of the BT. The selected workload should be representative of real workloads applied to the SUB and also portable, especially when comparing different benchmark targets.

The **Faultload** consists of a set of faults and exceptional conditions that are intended to emulate the real threats the system would experience. Faults are applied to one or more components of the SUB (different from the BT) which constitute the *Fault Injection Target (FIT)*. The reliability of the dependability measures carried out by a dependability benchmark is strictly related with the representativeness of the selected faultload. Many relevant works have been published on dependability benchmarking, focusing on several classes of systems. As for OSs, their dependability has been benchmarked with respect to faulty drivers [37] and with respect to application faults [51, 52, 53]. In the former case software faults are injected into a particular driver, according to a "commonly observed" distribution of these faults, whereas in the latter case faults are injected into the interface between the OS and the application, by corrupting system call parameters.

Server applications (DBMS, OLTP,HTTP, ...) has also been benchmarked [54, 55]: software faults are usually injected directly into the OS system class. OS profilers are employed to select the System Calls in which faults should be injected. Therefore the OS plays as the FIT and the server application as the BT.

In [27], the specific problem of software faults with respect to dependability benchmarking is addressed for the first time. IN particular, the authors recognize that the most critical task of a dependability benchmark is the definition of a portable, repeatable and representative fault-load. These properties are required to achieve the standardization of the benchmark but they are very hard to get in the case of software faults. The authors propose a new methodology for the definition of faultloads based on software faults for dependability benchmarking, which are not tied to any specific software vendor or platform, The work is based on *G-SWFIT* and the properties of the generated faultloads are analyzed and validated through experimentation using a case study of dependability benchmarking of web-servers.

Chapter 2

The DLR framework

Software faults can manifest transiently, especially during the operational phase of the target system. This means that transient manifestations of these faults cannot be discriminated as in traditional diagnosis approaches. Furthermore, this hampers the definition of an exhaustive fault model at design time. In the context of mission and safety critical systems, it is crucial to recover promptly from these faults in order to avoid mishaps. Hence, a novel diagnosis approach is needed in charge of encompassing transient manifestation of software faults, and of triggering effective recovery actions to let the system work properly. This chapter is going to (i) introduce the need for a novel approach and (ii), to explain the one which is proposed in this thesis. It is is made up of a Detection, a Location and a Recovery phase (DLR framework).

2.1 The need for DLR

The presence of software faults and their transient way of manifest prevent to define the system fault model at design/development time completely. This means that faults can manifest during the operational life of the system. Such faults never occurred during the pre-release testing and debugging phases, which are far from being exhaustive due to the software size and complexity. The failures which result from these unexpected faults, known as *production run failures* or *field failures* (e.g., crashes, hangs and incorrect results), are the major contributors to system downtime and dependability pitfalls [56]. While high availability requirements, which govern both mission and business critical systems, require the system downtime to be minimized, dependability pitfalls have to be warded off in order to avoid catastrophic failures. To pursue these goals, it is necessary to face *field failures* by (i) locating where they come from and (ii), by recovering the system through fast and proper recovery actions. In other words, *a recovery oriented diagnosis is needed to preserve system availability and to reduce the risk of mishaps (i.e., catastrophic failures).*

Traditionally, diagnosis has been conceived as the process of identifying the root cause of a failure i.e., it aimed solely to go up to the origin of the failure starting from its outward symptoms. These symptoms were assumed as a given truth, i.e., the detection mechanisms which signaled them were not a matter of interest for diagnosis. In the case of hardware systems, for which it is possible to draw a complete fault model at design/development time, this is a very effective approach in that detectors could be designed at that time as well. Unfortunately, this does not hold for software faults, which make the fault model of a system evolving over time. Hence, the detection has to be included into the diagnosis process, i.e., a novel approach has to be designed in charge of making detectors aware of errors which can manifest on the field. The first attempt to combine detection and location to perform fault diagnosis has been made by Vaidya et al.in [10], where the problem of distributed systems recovery from a large number of faults was addressed. The authors demonstrate that by combining detection and location adaptively, the number of diagnosed faults increases at a low additional cost.

Most of the previous work which has been conducted on software faults diagnosis in the last few

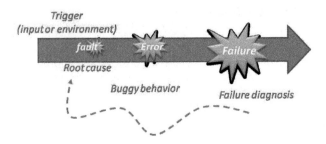

Figure 2.1: Fault propagation

years proposed off-line diagnosis approaches. These approaches, which require human involvement to discover the bug, are not suitable for field failures for a number of reasons. First of all,
it is difficult to reproduce failure-triggering conditions in house in order to perform diagnosis.
Second, off-line failure diagnosis cannot provide timely guidance to select a recovery action
which is tailored for the particular fault that occurred. Last, but more important, the time
to recover has to be minimized for the sake of availability and safety. Figure 2.1 shows how
a fault can manifest in a failure. Triggering conditions, which have been introduced by ODC
(see section 1.2.4), can activate a fault depending on the execution environment, as well as on
load conditions. Traditional testing and debugging techniques, as well as static code analysis,
aim to discover software bugs by means of a "blind" code screening. Although useful information about errors and failures can be gathered by means of this screening, there is no way to
understand the propagation path, i.e., what is the root cause of the discovered error/failure.
Conversely, the problem of diagnosis is driven by the occurrence of a given failure and it aims to
trace its origin in terms of (i) what are the execution misbehaviors which caused its occurrence
(ii), where these misbehaviors come from and (iii), what are the triggering conditions which
activated the fault.

2.2 System model and assumptions

In this thesis, diagnosis is going to be performed on complex software systems, deployed on several nodes and in charge of communicating through a network infrastructure. Each node oe the system is organized in software layers and it is made up of several *Diagnosable Units* (*DUs*), representing *atomic* software entities, at it is shown in Figure 2.2. In most of the cases the

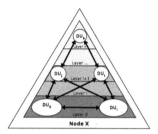

Figure 2.2: System's node model

layered structure of each node encompasses the Operating System (OS), the Middleware and the User Application levels. Such a structure has been used in this thesis as it focuses on software faults, rather than on hardware threats, thus the underlying hardware equipment has not been taken into account. This assumption sounds reasonable since modern systems are equipped with redundant and highly reliable hardware platforms which are developed and extensively tested in house, especially in the case of mission and safety critical systems. This means that hardware related faults will be not diagnosed by the DLR framework proposed in this thesis. However, hardware faults are very likely to be confined within the hardware/firmware levels by the high-performance hardware treatment built-in mechanisms.

DUs are assumed to be OS processes. This means that a process is the smallest entity which can be affected by a failure, and for which it is possible to diagnose faults, as well as to trigger recovery actions. Of course, the bug which caused the process to fail can be located within

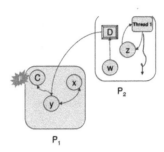

Figure 2.3: Diagnosis at process level.

an OTS library or module which is being executed in the context of the process; additionally, propagations can occur among different nodes and layers. Look at Figure 2.3, where the process P_1 experiences a failure due to the component C. However, the failure is actually located into the D library, which is running in the context of a different process, P_2 and the bug propagates to C through y, e.g., due to an erroneous input from D to y. According to a recovery oriented perspective, addressing the process as the atomic entity of the system, it is enough to identify the cause which induced the failure of the process, within the context of the process itself. In other words, if a recovery action has been defined in charge of recovering the failed process by only acting on it, it is unnecessary to go back through the propagation chain out of the context of the process. From Figure 2.3, the failure of P_1 will be attributed to y, which is the last link in the propagation within the P_1 context. Once the root cause has been identified, the proper recovery action has to be selected. Hence, the final output of diagnosis consists of a couple of vectors (D, R). The former associates the failed node, by means of the IP address, to the failed process which is identified by the Process ID (PID). The latter, instead, associates the experienced failure (f) to the recovery action to be initiated (r). Schematically

$$D = (IP_{failednode}, PID_{failedprocess})$$

$$R = (Failure_f, Recovery_r)$$

The diagnosis output provides information about the failed process, rather than about the component which caused the failure. This information would not be interesting for the final users. However, it could be helpful for bug fixing and fault removal.

Crash, hangs and workload failures are encompassed by the proposed approach. A process crash is the unexpected interruption of its execution due either to an external or an internal error. A process hang, instead, can be defined as a stall of the process. Hangs can be due to several causes, such as deadlock, livelock or waiting conditions on busy shared resources. As for workload failures, they depend on the running application. Workload failures can be both value- (e.g., erroneous output provided by a function) or timing failures.

Since the target systems are distributed on several nodes, and since faults can propagate, the set of the failures to be encompassed is given by $FM = FxDUs$, i.e., by the product set of the failure types and of all the DUs (i.e., the processes).

2.2.1 Recovery Actions

The proposed DLR framework encompasses two classes of recovery actions:

- **System Level Recovery**, i.e., actions which aim to repair a failed process by acting at system level. These actions are intended for dealing with crashes and hangs, and they can be more or less costly depending on the size of the system, as well as on the number of processes involved into the failure. Encompassed actions are system reboot, application restart and process kill. Once one of these actions has been performed, additional facilities, e.g. fault tolerance mechanisms provided by the middleware layer, will be able to restore the application.

- **Workload Level Recovery**, i.e., action which aim to repair application failures. These actions are intended for dealing with workload failures, hence a knowledge of the application semantic is required, as well as of its business logic.

2.3 The overall approach

Figure 2.4 gives an overall picture of the proposed approach, representing how it works from the fault occurrence till system recovery.

During the operational phase of the system, a monitoring system performs continuous detection. Once a failure (F) has occurred, an alarm is triggered which does initiate the Location phase. During the location, the root cause of the failure is looked for; once this has been completed, the Recovery phase is started in order to recover the system and to resume normal activities. Let L_d, L_l and L_r be the times required for performing detection, location and recovery, respectively. This means that the entire DLR process will be completed in $L = L_d + L_l + L_r$, at worst. The task of detection consists of the alarm triggering when a given process fails. Since the failure of the overall system is not a certain consequence of a process failure, i.e., if a process fails it is not assured that the system will fail as well, a process failure is conceived as an error for the system as a whole. For this reason, the task of detection is in fact *error detection*.

The overall approach is based on the machine learning paradigm, as in many previous papers focusing on diagnosis [57, 58, 59]. The main reason for this is the presence of field failures, which cannot be known at design/development time. Indeed, such a paradigm makes the DLR engine, and all of its components, able to learn over time. Hence, field failures influence the

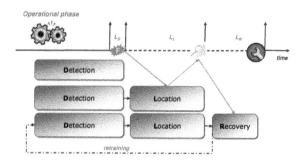

Figure 2.4: A time snapshot of the overall DLR approach

design of the entire engine, from detection to recovery.

As for detection, an error is defined as a corruption in the state of a DU, which can impact in turn on the state of the system. An alarm is triggered whenever an anomaly is encountered in system behavior; this is achieved by means of anomaly detection, i.e., all the conditions which deviate from *normal* behaviors are labeled as *errors*. This is quite a pessimistic detection strategy. In fact, not all the anomalies correspond to actual errors, i.e., errors could be signaled even when the system is behaving correctly but that condition has not been recognized as normal. On the one hand, such a pessimistic strategy leads to a non negligible amount of false positives, in that alarms are likely to be triggered which do not correspond to actual errors. On the other hand, it allows to minimize the number of errors which is misinterpreted as normal behaviors, thus going unnoticed. This is crucial in the context of critical systems in that unsignaled errors are in fact false negatives which may have catastrophic effects. It is worth noting that reducing false positives, i.e., maximizing detection accuracy, at design time has been the primary goal to be pursued for the most of the previous work focusing on fault/errors detection. Details about the detection strategy, as well as about the architecture of the detection module will be given in chapter 3.

Once an alarm has been triggered, the Location phase is initiated to identify its root cause. Along with the aim of pinpointing the actual fault, this phase has also to remedy detection falls. More precisely, during this phase the presence of an actual fault has to be established, since false positives are likely to be triggered by the detectors. This means that the location module behaves "distrustfully" to compensate the pessimistic detection. This is achieved by the means of the machine learning paradigm, in the form of classification. Indeed, classification and pattern recognition methods are viable, if no further knowledge is available for the relationships between the errors (i.e., the features) and the faults. The features are determined experimentally for certain faults. The relation between features and faults is therefore learned (or trained) experimentally, and then stored thus forming an explicit knowledge base. Faults can be concluded by comparing of the observed features with the nominal feature. Starting from manifestations (i.e., the errors), the location module has to infer the presence of a fault and to associate it to a class. To design the fault classes properly, three circumstances has to be considered:

1. **SUSPECTED ERROR (SE)**: the triggered alarm was not the manifestation of an actual fault, i.e., detectors triggered a false positive. In this case, there is no need neither for location nor for system recovery;

2. **ERROR**: a fault actually occurred that the location module is able to identify. In this case, recovery actions have to be associated to the fault and initiated immediately;

3. **UNKNOWN FAULT**: the triggered alarm was actually due to a fault which cannot be identified during the location. This is the tricky case of a fault which is *unknown*, i.e., a fault that never occurred before. In this case, the system has to be put in a safe state, and further investigations are needed which can even require human intervention.

The location capability of uncovering false positives allows to improve the detection accuracy. This is the main goal of the feedback branch, named "retraining", depicted in Figure 2.4: once an alarm has been labeled as a SE, the detection module is upgraded consequently. This will allow to reduce the number of false positives over time, as well as the quality of the overall DLR process, as it will be shown in chapter 5. Of course, the frequency of detection module updates has to be established depending on its complexity. This is likely to depend on the classifier being used, as well as on the communication mechanisms between the location and the detection module. Hence, despite of the generality of the process, operations have to be planned according to the particular system under study.

The process of classification, along with the details about the classifiers used to perform location, will be described in chapter 5.

Recovery actions to be initiated in the case of an ERROR have been associated to the fault classes. This is to perform recovery actions which are tailored for the particular fault that occurred. This is a novel idea in field of faults diagnosis: to the best of author knowledge this has not been proposed yet in the literature.

Since the approach is intended for operational systems, two main phases are encompassed. During the first phase, the DLR engine is trained in order to build a *starting knowledge*. This corresponds to a preoperational phase of the system, used to setup and tune the engine properly. The knowledge built this way is leveraged during the second phase, i.e., the operational phase of the target system. Figure 2.5 depicts the training process. In order to train the detection module, which performs anomaly detection, faulty free executions (i.e., correct executions) of the system have to be run in order to model its normal behavior (1). Conversely, fault injection (2) is required in order to allow (i) the definition of the fault classes (3.a) and (ii), the collection and analysis of fault related data to model system behavior in faulty conditions (3.b). *DUs* running into the system, which are depicted as little triangles in the Figure, are the injection

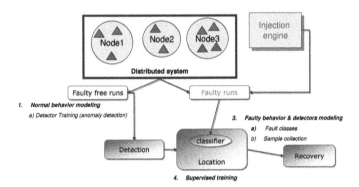

Figure 2.5: Training of the DLR engine

target. Once faults have been injected, the supervised training[1] of the location classifier is performed (4), according to the pseudo-algorithm in Figure 2.6. At the end of the training phase, both the detection and the location classifiers can rely on a starting knowledge about the target system. On the one hand this can be exploited during the operational phase. On the other hand, the base knowledge has to be improved during the system lifetime adaptively in order to take fields failures into account.

2.4 Related Work

The issue of diagnosis has been being faced since a long time, maybe since computers came. The first attempt to formalize the problem is due to Preparata et al. which introduced system level diagnosis in [12]. Since then, diagnosis has been faced by following several approaches and in many research fields: although significant progresses have been done, the problem is still far

---

[1]Details about this learning strategy are provided in chapter 5

```
FOR each node i
       FOR all the processes j running on i
            FOR each fault location k into the code of (i,j)
                   failure= do_injection(fault,k,i,j)
          //do the injection , wait for a while then analyze failed processes
                   IF (failure ==UNKNOWN)      {
                          ADD fault to the set of KNOWN faults
                          ASSOCIATE recovery mean to the injected fault
                   ENDIF
                   COLLECT data from detector related to the last D seconds
                       CREATE the entry (detector_ouput, failure)
                   ADD the entry to the training set
            ENDFOR
       ENDFOR
   ENDFOR

FOR each collected entry
     do_supervised_training(classifier)
ENDFOR
```

Figure 2.6: Supervised training of the location classifier

away from the solution.

The model they proposed in 1967 (also known as the PMC model) assumed the system to be made up of several units which test one another, and test results are leveraged to diagnose faulty units. Several extensions to this model have been proposed, even recently (e.g., [60] where the safe system level diagnosis has been proposed by Vaydia et al.)

In the last decade or so, there has being an increasing work focusing on the diagnosis problem which is getting faced by several perspectives, and by means of quite different techniques from a variety of research fields. On the one hand, such a generous literature is a benefit in that approaches and techniques exist which can be leveraged and improved with respect to the particular domain. On the other hand, this can be disorienting and drawing a systematic picture of the existing literature becomes an hard task. The bibliographic analysis conducted in the context of this thesis was aimed at giving a more clear overview of the available research results, by identifying similarities and divergences among the existing works, as well as with the approach proposed in the thesis.

2.4.1 Similar approaches to similar problems (SASP)

The goal of identifying the root cause of a failure automatically is pursued in [57]. Authors propose a trace-based problem diagnosis methodology, which relies on the trace of low level system behaviors to deduce problems of computer systems. Transient events occurring in the system (e.g., system calls, I/O requests, call stacks, context switches) are traced in order to (i) identify the correlations between system behaviors and known problems and (ii), use the learned knowledge to solve new coming problems. This goals are achieved by means of statistical learning techniques, based on Support Vector Machines (SVMs), as it is proposed in this thesis. The ultimate aim that authors want to pursue is to make the problem identification fully automatic, thus eliminating human involvement. The goal which is pursued in this thesis is different, in that the trigger of recovery actions is also considered. Furthermore, the symptom of the problem needs to be reproduced before the root cause detection.

A decision tree based approach is presented in [58] to diagnose problems in Large Internet Services. Similarly to what this thesis proposes, runtime properties of the system (they record clients requests) are monitored; automated machine learning and data mining techniques are used to identify the causes of failures. The proposed approach is evaluated by measuring precision and recall, the two most used metric which have been considered in this thesis too for evaluating diagnosis quality. However, the point which makes this work different in spirit from this thesis, concerns with detection. In fact, detection is not encompassed in [58]: authors assume problems to have been already detected and they only concentrate on identifying the root cause, in order to trigger a fast recovery.

2.4.2 Similar approaches to different problems (SADP)

[61] proposes automated support for classifying reported software failures in order to facilitate the diagnosing of their root causes. The authors use a classification strategy which makes use of supervised and unsupervised pattern classification , as it is done in this thesis for location and detection respectively. Additionally, they also concentrate on the importance of features selection and extraction. However, the classification performed in this work aims to group failures which are due to the same cause and it is conceived as a mean for helping actual diagnosis. Conversely, in this thesis diagnosis is actually performed by means of classification. A very recent work which uses a machine learning approach based on SVM classification is [62]. Its main goal is to predict the presence of latent software bugs in software changes (change classification). In particular, a machine learning SVM classifier is used to determine whether a new software change is more similar to prior buggy changes or clean changes. In this manner, change classification predicts the existence of bugs in software changes. The work shares with this thesis the classification problem and its formulation.

Machine learning approach has also been used in [59] for identifying program properties that indicate errors. The technique generates machine learning models of program properties known to result from errors, and applies these models to program properties of user-written code to classify the properties that may lead the user to errors. SVMs and decision trees are used for classification. The effectiveness of the proposed approach has been demonstrated with respect to C, C++, and Java programs. However it requires human labor to find the bugs, and the process is not fully automatic.

Aguilera et al. [63] address the problem of locating performance bottlenecks in a distributed system with only internode communication traces. They infer the causal paths through multi-tier distributed applications from message level traces, in order to detect the node causing extraordinary delay. They share with this thesis the great attention which is paid to the presence of OTS items, as well as the fact that the approach requires no modifications to applications and middleware. The major differences concern (i) the fact that the pay more attention to performance rather than on faults and (ii), the fact that they perform off-line diagnosis of the problem.

As for Bayesian estimation, a worth noting work to be referred is [64] which addresses system diagnosis problems. It refers to comparison-based system analysis to deal with incomplete test coverage, unknown numbers of faulty units, and non-permanent faults. However, only one type of monitor is used in that work and also recovery is not encompassed.

2.4.3   Different approaches to similar problems (DASP)

Closely related to the goals of this thesis are the aims of [13], which cares automatic model driven recovery in distributed systems. Similarly to what this thesis proposes for detection, authors exploit a set of a limited coverage monitors whose output are combined in a certain way prior to trigger recovery actions. Additionally they also have a Bayesian Faults Diagnosis engine in charge of locating the problem, as well as to pilot a recovery controller that can choose recovery actions based on several optimization criteria. Similarly to what is proposed here, the approacj described in [13] is able to detect whether a problem is beyond its diagnosis and recovery capabilities, and thus to determine when a human operator needs to be alerted. Despite of these common purposes, this thesis takes an opposite perspective, in that a model based approach has been discarded: modeling complex software systems could be too difficult and inaccurate for the purposes of diagnosis. Additionally, this thesis work is different in several points. First, authors of [13] propose incremental recovery actions whereas here the best one action able to repair the system is started directly. Second, here the entire set of "always-on" monitors is always used detect errors instead of invoking additional monitors when needed, as they do. Third, fault injection has been used in this thesis to experimentally prove the effectiveness of the approach rather than for making a comparison with a theoretical optimum. This has not been encompassed in [13].

[65] deals with the problem of diagnosis in networked environments made up of black-box entities. This goal is achieved by (i) tracing messages to build a causal dependency structure between the components (ii), by tracing back the causal structure when a failure is detected and (iii), by testing components using diagnostic tests. Runtime observations are used to estimate the parameters that bear on the possibility of error propagation, such as unreliability of links and error masking capabilities. The work aims to provide diagnosis of the faulty entities at runtime in a non-intrusive manner to the application. Differently from this work, in this thesis a causal structure of the system is not built since any assumptions on the structure of the system itself is made. The main point in common is the fact is the on-line diagnosis strategy.

[66] defines a methodology for identifying and characterizing dynamic dependencies between system components in distributed application environments, which relies on active perturbation of the system. This is in order to identify dependencies, as well as to compute dependency strengths. Even if discovering system dependencies automatically could be a good way for root cause analysis, it is assumed a deep knowledge of the dynamics of the system dynamics. In particular, authors assume to completely know end-users interaction with the system (they use a well known TPC benchmark). The opposite position is taken by this thesis, in that knowledge is not required. Furthermore, the Active Dependency Discovery approach defined in that work, is strongly intrusive and workload dependent.

A further worth referring work is [67], where the Pinpoint framework is defined. It employs statistical learning techniques to diagnose failures in a Web farm environment. After the traces with respect to different client requests are collected, data mining algorithms are used to identify the components most relevant to a failure. This thesis shares with that work the "learning from system behavior" philosophy. However, there is a difference in goals, the faults detection and diagnosis are performed in order to determine the cause of the failure and trigger recovery action. Conversely, Pinpoint aims to recognize which component in a distributed system is more likely to be faulty. Fault injection is used also in [67] to prove the effectiveness of the approach. The major limitation of this approach are that (i) it is suitable only for small scale software programs, and (ii) it exhibit a significant logging. The approach proposed in this thesis differs from that work in two main points: (i) the Pinpoint framework is designed to work off-line and (ii), it is not a recovery-oriented approach.

Finally, on-site failure diagnosis is faced in [56]. The work aims to capture the failure point and conduct just-in-time failure diagnosis with checkpoint and re-execution system support. Lightweight checkpoints are taken during execution and rolls back are performed to recent checkpoints for diagnosis after a failure has occurred. Delta generation and delta analysis are exploited to speculatively modify the inputs and execution environment to create many similar but successful and failing replays to identify failure-triggering conditions. Such an approach has been discarded in this thesis since Heisenbugs (and even worse Mandelbugs [23]) can be unreproducible this way: in fact, their conditions of activation are hard to identify. Furthermore, long time is required (almost five minutes) to complete the process: this can be not tolerable for safety critical systems.

Table 2.1: Related work summary

REF	CAT	OBJ	TECHNIQUE
[57]	SASP	Root Cause Analysis	Machine Learning (SVM)
[61]	SADP	Software failures automatic classification	Pattern identification in execution profiles
[13]	DASP	Detection, location and recovery	Model based; Bayesian/Markov estimation
[62]	SADP SADP	Latent software bugs prediction	Machine Learning (SVM)
[65]	DASP	Arbitrary Failures Probabilistic Diagnosis	Runtime observation messages propagation
[58]	SASP	Recovery Oriented Failure Diagnosis	Runtime trace Logging; Machine learning (Dec.tree)
[59]	SADP	Latent software bugs discovery	Machine Learning (SVM;Dec. Tree); Dynamic Analysis
[66]	DASP	Root cause analysis	Active Dynamic Dependencies
[63]	SADP	Testing/Debugging; Performance bottlenecks isolation	Message tracing; Causal Pattern Identification
[67]	DASP	Root Cause Analysis; Automatic Problem Identification	Message tracing; Data mining and clustering
[56]	DASP	Production failures on site diagnosis; Testing/debugging	Checkpointing; rollback; Static and dynamic analysis

Chapter 3

Faults and Error Detection

This chapter aims to illustrate the detection approach proposed in this thesis. It leverages the OS support to detect application failures, which could be not properly detected otherwise. In fact, it allows to detect failures which manifest as kernel hangs, even being generated at application level, and which are not detected by the application and middleware built-in mechanisms in many cases. The kernel self-detection capability, i.e., its ability to detect kernel hangs, have been investigated in order to quantify its trustworthiness. Notwithstanding the effectiveness of the kernel detection means, some deficiencies emerged, hence a detection algorithm has been implemented to improve their quality. The overall detection architecture, aiming to detect application failures, is composed of several monitors, whose responses have been combined by a global detector. The implemented algorithm for kernel hangs detection has been used as a monitor, thus making the system in charge of detecting application failures which manifest at OS the level and improving the overall detection quality.

The terminology

In this thesis, detection has been faced at different levels, from the lowermost one, the OS, to the uppermost, i.e., the applications. Hereafter we refer to error detection: it aims is to detect errors prior them to degenerate into failures for other system components, or for the overall system.

3.1 Existing approaches to the problem of detection

Two main lines have been followed in the literature for coping with the problem of detection. The former is a theoretical line, that tries to give a formalization of the problem, especially for what concerns with quality evaluation. The milestone work in this context is [68], that studies the quality of service (QoS) of failure detectors in message-passing distributed systems in which processes may fail by crashing, and messages may be delayed or dropped by communication links. By failure, it is meant a process crash in these systems. The quality of the detection quantifies (a) how fast the failure detector detects actual failures[1], and (b) how well it avoids false detections. Latency and accuracy metrics are associated to these measures, respectively. The latter line, instead, addresses the problem of detection empirically, taking the QoS topics addressed in [68] as a reference point for validating systems and mechanisms.

Following this line, detection strategies can be implemented as local or remote detection modules, depending on whether they are or not deployed on the same node of the monitored component. Local and remote detection can be implemented with query-based or log-based techniques. Query-based techniques rely on interrogating the monitored entity health status, to discover potential anomalies. The query can be performed periodically (heartbeat techniques, such as [69, 70]), or implicitly each time another distributed entity tries to invoke the

---

[1] we refer to failures as the authors do that in this work

monitored one [68].

Log-based techniques, instead, consist in analyzing the log files produced by the entity, if available [71, 72]. In fact, these may contain many useful data to understand the system dependability behavior, as shown by many studies on the field [73, 74]. Moreover, logs are the only direct source of information available in the case of OTS items.

Both query-based and log-based techniques can be considered as direct detection techniques: they try to infer the entity health status by directly querying it, or by analyzing data items it is able to log. A different approach lies into infer the health of the observed entity by monitoring its behavior from an external viewpoint, along with its interactions with the environment. These approaches can be labeled as indirect detection techniques. As an example, the work in [75] exploits hardware performance counters and OS signals to monitor the system behavior and to signal possible anomalous conditions. A similar approach is followed in [76], which provides detection facilities for large scale distributed systems running legacy code. The detection system proposed here is an autonomous self checking monitor, which is architecture independent and it has a hierarchical structure. The monitors are designed to observe the external messages that are exchanged between the protocol entities of the distributed system under study. They use the observed messages to deduce a runtime state transition diagram (STD) that has been executed by the all the entities in the system.

Indirect techniques have been especially adopted for intrusion detection systems. In these cases, anomaly detection approaches are used to compare normal and anomalous runs of the system. In [77] the execution of a program is characterized by tracing patterns of invoked system calls. System call traces produced in the operational phase are then compared with nominal traces to reveal intrusion conditions.

Other solutions, such as [78, 79], are based on data mining approaches, such as document classification. They extract recurrent execution patterns (using system calls or network connections) to model the application under nominal conditions, and to classify run-time behaviors as normal or anomalous. Such solutions are able to achieve high quality, in terms of all the metrics we defined in section 3.2. However, they require high computational load due to the huge amount of collected data. They have been widely used to detect intrusions: to the best of our knowledge, they have not been applied to transient software faults yet.

All these solutions are not intended for diagnosis. They work as autonomous detection systems, hence they do not have location in mind. Additionally, none of them faces the problem of transient software faults, which are the trickiest issue in the context of complex OTS based software systems. This is especially true in the case of complex concurrent applications, where multi-threading and shared resources represent a source of nondeterminism in the application behavior, at execution time. In these systems, detection has to take place during the operational phase of the system (i.e., on-line). For these reasons, both direct application level techniques (such as polling the health status of system components via heartbeat) and log based techniques fail when dealing with these systems. On the one hand, the implementation of simple heartbeat schemes generally requires extra code. On the other hand, log-based detection typically requires a significant computational load to be performed on-line; for instance data mining techniques are used often. Furthermore, direct techniques may result inadequate at detecting software hangs. These are usually due to synchronization faults (that are in fact Heisenbugs), and they manifest as infinite loops (active hangs) or indefinite wait conditions (passive hangs). First, the hang might be localized on a different thread than the one that answers to the heartbeat. Hence, the entity correctly answers to polls, while portions of it result permanently hang. Second, it is hard to tell whether it does not respond to queries or it does not log any data because it is really hang or it is just "very slow" (e.g., it might be overloaded or correctly blocked on a waiting condition).

Indirect detection techniques, that have been recently introduced in the literature, allow to overcome these limitations. The system is observed through low level parameters related to the entity of interest (e.g., invoked system calls, hardware performance counters), in order to build a model of the correct or expected behavior of the system. In this thesis, an indirect detection approach is proposed, as it is detailed in the rest of this chapter.

3.2   Detection quality metrics

In order to evaluate the effectiveness of detection mechanisms and strategies, as well as to make comparisons among different approaches, quality metrics are defined. The two main metrics which are generally used in this context, i.e., latency and accuracy, have been defined in [68] (see section3.1).

In this thesis, these two metrics have been used, along with a third metric, the Coverage C_{det}, which takes into account the number of events which are properly detected. This is mainly due to the fact the reference failure model encompasses failures which are more difficult to detect than crash failures (which are usually the only failures taken into account) hence, there is a non zero probability of having undetected failures. Formally, we follow:

1. Detection accuracy, i.e., the percentage of detected events which actually occurred. It is the detector ability to avoid false positives.

2. Detection coverage, i.e., the detector capacity to uncover failures. It can be measured as the number of detected failures divided by the overall number of failures which actually occurred.

3. Detection latency, i.e., the time between the occurrence of the event and its detection.

3.3   The role of the Operating System

The intuition behind the detection approach proposed in this thesis, is that the OS can be leveraged to overcome the limitations of the detection approaches which have been proposed so far to detect application failures.

As discussed in section 3.1, direct techniques are the most common. They place the observation mean at the same level they want to observe, e.g., they try to detect applications/middleware errors by using the logs provided by the application/middleware itself. This has serious limitations. First, some events may cause the system to get blocked completely, thus excluding the possibility of exploiting built-in detection mechanisms. In other words, if the system is hang, the process in charge of detection may get hang too, thus being unable of providing useful information. Second, some events could be the effect of low level causes, i.e., of faults located under the observation point (e.g., application failures due to an error in the middleware), hence they could be not "visible" to the observer (as depicted by the blue arrows in Figure 3.1). Last,

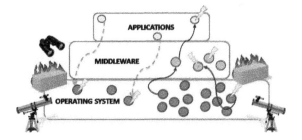

Figure 3.1: Indirect detection techniques observation point of view.

but most important, *there are application failures which can manifest at OS level in the form of kernel hangs* (the green arrows in Figure 3.1). Hence, they can only be detected by observing the system by the OS point of view.

Query-based techniques, that do not suffer such limitations, require extra code to be added into the monitored module in order to answer to queries, that is not feasible for OTS items. This is overcome by log-based techniques which, however, are usually computationally inefficient, hence they are not effective for on-line detection. Furthermore, they are complicated by the heterogeneity of log files, as OTS items produce log files with different formats.

For these reasons, the detection approach proposed in this thesis is based on an indirect detection technique.

3.4 Operating system self-detection capabilities

As OSs play a key role in the detection process, in that they support upper layers detection mechanisms, their self-detection capabilities (i.e., the ability of detecting their own failures) have to be investigated. Indeed, OS logs represent the most valuable way to detect erroneous states of a complex, OTS-based, system, as well as an effective mean to catch application failures which manifest into the kernel. Such logs have been exploited as the main detection mean in [80] for failure prediction, and in [4] for fault diagnosis and treatment. However, several studies uncovered logging deficiencies in the most famous OSs such as [74], which pointed out that information about the cause of Windows NT OS reboots were not provided in many cases, and [81, 82], where it has been demonstrated that OS logs can even be misleading, as they can provide false detections.

In this thesis, kernel logging capabilities of the Linux OS have been investigated in order to decide whether a critical system can actually rely on them, or some additional facilities are needed to perform a high quality detection.

3.4.1 Kernel failure modes

Kernel failures can be broadly classified in Kernel Hangs (KHs) and Kernel Panics (KPs). The former can occur in two cases. First, a KH is experienced when the kernel is blocked in an infinite loop, or it is waiting for an event that will never occur, and interrupts are disabled. Hence, the system is completely stalled. In this case, both applications and other software modules interacting with the kernel are no longer served. Second, KHs can occur which do not cause the system to be completely blocked. In this case, one or more applications are caused to be indefinitely waiting for a given event, either in kernel- (i.e., the application waits for the completion of a stalled system call) or in user-space (i.e., the application is misbehaving due to incorrect return values or other side-effects of the system call API). KPs occur when the OS detects an internal fatal error from which it cannot safely recover by means of hardware exceptions (e.g., when an invalid memory address is accessed or when an hardware failure occur). In this case, a panic handler routine is called which is in charge of providing diagnostic messages (e.g., a dump of the stack and CPU registers) to the connected terminals, to allow post-mortem analysis. Then, the system is stopped to prevent further damages as the system would be in an unstable, erroneous, state: a (manual or automatic) reboot is the only way to resume system execution. Thus, the kernel is able to notify such failures in most of the cases. Conversely, hangs are hardly ever notified by the kernel itself, because the error state is not explicitly signaled by hardware exceptions, hence they become the major concern.

3.4.2 Evaluation of kernel logging capabilities

Software faults have been injected into the kernel source code aiming to evaluate the logging capabilities of the Linux OS. To be more clear, the ultimate aim of the performed injection campaign is to evaluate to what extent the *built-in* logging mechanisms are able to provide error notifications prior the kernel to fail.

By software fault, it is meant a software defect, which in fact corresponds to a bug into the code. An error occurs if the fault is activated. It represents an erroneous state of the system (e.g., a wrong value into a memory register) which can lead to a failure if it propagates to the system interface, i.e. to the kernel interface with either external modules or applications. As fault injection has been used recurrently throughout all this thesis, it has been thoroughly faced in section 1.2.8.

Software Mutation (*SM*) has been applied (i.e., faults have been injected into the kernel source code directly, see section 1.2.8). This is mainly for the sake of representativeness, as it is crucial to evaluate detection capabilities with respect to faults which are likely to occur in practice. For this reason, the fault model is based on field data, and it is realistic in terms of *what* and *where* to inject. It has been achieved by analyzing several public forums and newsgroups from where discussions about kernel hangs experienced by Linux developers and skilled users have been selected. The analysis revealed that:

- infinite waits on locks are by far the most frequent cause of hangs within the kernel. *Spinlocks* (i.e., exclusive locks in which a CPU is in active waiting) are the most used synchronization mean;

- Hangs are often due to threads within the kernel trying to acquire a lock which is already held [2];

- Kernel subsystems can hang due to interrupts handling code, e.g., interrupts are masked when the kernel is waiting for a device-driven event[3];

- Kernel hang can be caused by wrong handling of a set of multiple locks, e.g., locks

---

[2]http://lwn.net/Articles/261271
[3]http://thread.gmane.org/gmane.linux.kernel/286491, http://lwn.net/Articles/138165

related to page tables and memory areas should be both acquired to perform memory management[4];

- Defects can be due to wrong assumptions about locks held when executing a piece of code, e.g., a function should not be called without prior holding a specific lock[5].

From these observations, a *fault library* has been designed consisting of the following classes:

- Missing release of a spinlock got before, e.g., within a function (*F1*);

- Locking of two or more spinlocks in reverse order; this can result into a so-called 'A-B-B-A' deadlock situation (*F2*);

- Missing unlock/lock operations on a spinlock within a given piece of code (*F3*);

- Interrupts re-enabling omission when exiting a critical section in which they were disabled (*F4*).

The fault library has been realized both by omitting some pieces of kernel code, and by modifying it in several points. This is to emulate *missing* and *wrong* constructs, which have been demonstrated to account for the majority of actual faults [1].

Representativeness in terms of *"where"* to injects, has been achieved by profiling the invocations of the functions which make use of spinlocks; this required to instrument the kernel. Then, faults have been injected into those primitives for that, during the execution of a workload (i) a given spinlock has been acquired more than 1000 times and (ii), a spinlock has been contended by other CPUs more than 100 times. This way it is quite likely to induce kernel hangs. However, the kernel code which is executed during a given experiment may vary, depending on the

---

[4]http://article.gmane.org/gmane.linux.kernel.mm/16003, http://lwn.net/Articles/130160
[5]http://lwn.net/Articles/274292

workload. For this reason, such a profiling has to be repeated prior to chose fault locations, for each workload.

3.4.3 Kernel logging deficiencies

Synthetic workloads, which are representative of the most common operations in the context of long running mission critical applications, has been used. Filebench [6], i.e., an Open Source suite for measuring and comparing filesystems performances, has been used to pursue this issue. Three different workloads encompassed by the suite have been used for experiments: (i)Varmail (**W1**), which emulates a Network File System mail server (ii), **Fileserver (W2)** which performs a sequence of file system operations (create, delete, append...) and (iii), Oltp (**W3**) which is a database emulator. This sounds reasonable in that the most common operations performed in mission critical scenarios fall within these categories, e.g., flight data plan exchanges in Air Traffic Control systems.

An experimental campaign has been conducted on a computer equipped with 2 Xeon 2.8GHz processors, 5Gb of RAM, and a 36 Gb SCSI hard disk (10000 RPM). Kernel version 2.6.25 has been used, and workloads have been generated by using Filebench version 1.64[7]. Dynamic probing has been used to monitor procedures execution and to inject faults by the means of *KProbes* and *SystemTap* tools (see details in section 3.5.3). Results in Figure 3.2 show that Linux mechanisms failed to detect hangs to significant extent. About the 25% of injected faults, resulted in KHs which have not been detected by the kernel. With respect to the metrics defined in section 3.2, this means that the kernel exhibited a coverage equal to 75%. This is a worrying result, that could be not tolerable in critical scenarios. Hence, a detection algorithm has been proposed in this thesis, which is able to improve the detection performances of the

---

[6]http://www.solarisinternals.com/wiki/index.php/FileBench
[7]http://www.cs.rice.edu/~gulati/

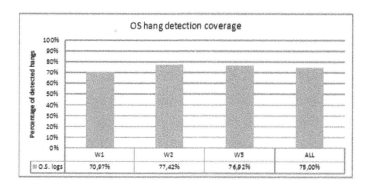

Figure 3.2: OS hang detection coverage. The 25% of the KHs has not been detected by the Linux kernel.

native Linux OS logging mechanisms, with respect to kernel hangs.

3.4.4 An algorithm for improving kernel hang detection

The algorithm is based on the continuous monitoring of the kernel I/O operations rate and it has been designed by taking in mind: (i) to keep the overhead low, and (ii) to propose a solution which is easy to be implemented.

By observing disk and network I/O throughput values, the algorithm is able to detect the presence of a failure in the system. I/O operations have been already used as a detection mean in several studies coming from different research fields [83, 84]. The results achieved by these works make reasonable to claim that monitoring the I/O operations rate can be very helpful into the detection of KHs, as experiments confirm (see section 3.4.5).

Failure free executions of a given workload into the target system exhibit a *regular* I/O operations rate, i.e., the number of I/O operations per second (throughput, *th*) ranges within an interval, $I = [I^-, I^+]$. This models the normal behavior of the system, and we assume deviations from such behavior as the symptom of a failure. As for example, if a thread is blocked due to a deadlock, the I/O operations it would have executed normally are not performed, thus inducing a *th* loss. Although this is a general statement, values for I, i.e., its lower and upper bounds, are strongly related to the running workload. Additionally, even in steady workloads (i.e., statistical characterization of I/O operations does not significantly change over time), fluctuations due to secondary factors, e.g., a temporary overload, can lead to *th* samples misinterpreted as failures (false positives). In fact, the proper definition of $[I^-, I^+]$ is the key to discriminate normal workload executions from anomalous ones. To get a correct definition of I, running workload has been modeled as a random process X, and by using a counter, C, which takes into account the *duration* of the *th* variation. More precisely, a parametric model of the workload is proposed, which is based on the computation of its first order statistics, i.e., the statistical average (m_X), and the standard deviation (σ_X). The workload is supposed to be a stationary random process, i.e., m_X and σ_X do not significantly change over time (i.e., for a long execution period). Real data from the field confirm that this is a reasonable assumption for long running and near-real time applications. Indeed, traffic data related to a Flight Data Plans (FDP) manager have been collected and analyzed, within the framework of an industrial collaborations with Selex-SI [8], a leading European company in the context of ATC. Data refer to the flight traffic at the Neapolitan Airport within a day[9]; statistical analysis pointed out that FDP management operations, as well as the number of departing and landing flights, exhibit first order statistic which do not significantly vary during 6 hours time slots, during daytime and the evening (see Table 3.1). A further example comes from Oracle DataBase Management

---

[8]COSMIC Project, http://www.cosmiclab.it

[9]Data comes from an industrial collaboration with SICTA Consortium, http://www.sicta.it

Systems [10], for which it has been observed a stationary aggregate behavior in several long running applications.

In order to model the normal behavior of the target application, the algorithm has to be

Table 3.1: Flight Data exhibit a stationary behavior within a day (30 days, excluding the nights).

TIME INTERVAL	ARRIVALS	MEAN DEPARTURES	OPERATIONS
06:00-12:00 A.M.	32.776	31.611	64.388
12:00 06:00 P.M.	37.278	39.111	76.386
06:00 12:00 P.M.	34.943	32.555	67.523
STD. DEV.	2.251	4.085	6.222

tuned properly. By running the workload in failure free conditions, m_X and σ_X are computed,
as well as the threshold values k^+, k^-. An upper bound, for C, i.e., the threshold values $\overline{C}$ (see
equation 3.1), is also tuned as follows:

$$
y = \begin{cases} 1 & \text{if } X(t) > m_X \text{ and } |X(t) - m_X| > k^+\sigma_X \\ 1 & \text{if } X(t) < m_X \text{ and } |X(t) - m_X| < k^-\sigma_X \\ 0 & \text{otherwise} \end{cases} \tag{3.1}
$$

During the operational phase of the system, th is periodically sampled by the detection algorithm, which compares each sample, $X(t)$, to the precomputed m_X. The failure detection is
performed in two steps. First, it has to be established whether the licit range for normal th
variation has been exceeded (equation 3.1). Second, short-time deviations are filtered out in
order to take into account licit workload fluctuations, due to secondary factors. The threshold
values k^+ and k^- define the licit range for th variations (they have to be set in order to minimize
false positives). The second step is performed by using the C counter, which is incremented if
the samples significantly differs from the average. Otherwise, its value is reset to zero. In other
words, $C=C+1$ if $y=1$; $C=0$ otherwise. A failure is actually detected, when $C > \overline{C}$. Note that

---

[10]http://www.nyoug.org/Presentations/SIG/DBA/dbasig_wlc1.pdf

(i) $\overline{C}$ has to be tuned preliminarily and (ii), that we use $k^-\sigma_X$ and $k^+\sigma_X$ to indicate the above mentioned bounds I^-, I^+. This is to explicitly take into account variations from m_X, i.e., the standard deviation.

Discussion. The hypotheses of a stationary workload has a limited validity. It can be relaxed to encompass workloads whose first order statistics change over time. This could be done by profiling the workload preliminarily, and by using a more complex model, such as a Hidden Markov Model (HMM). In this case, m_X and σ_X could be estimated for each sample, rather than using the same value for all the samples. Additionally, the HMM should be trained with respect to the *th* samples collected during the training phase. Then, depending on the state, different values for $\overline{C}$ and for the thresholds have to be enforced. Of course, this generalized version would require a greater implementation effort, and it is very likely to increase the overhead [85].

3.4.5   Results

In order to evaluate to what extent the proposed algorithm was able to improve detection quality, with respect to the metrics defined in section 3.2, it has been run under the workload described in section 3.4.3, in the same experimental conditions. As shown in Figure 3.3, it has been able to detect about the 94% of the hangs, thus exhibiting better coverage if compared to the native Linux mechanisms (which detected only the 75% of the faults). This holds both with respect to single workloads and to the entire set of experiments.

Table 3.2 summarizes the coverage values with respect to fault classes. The best results have been achieved with respect to classes $F1$ and $F2$, which are easier to detect (e.g., by means of a check into the function acquiring the lock) if compared to the other classes which are related to more complex situations, e.g., interrupts masking. As for detection latency, Figure 3.4 reports

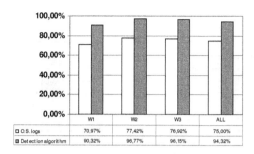

Figure 3.3: Detection algorithm coverage

Table 3.2: Coverage with respect to fault class and workloads

Type	Coverage			
	W1	W2	W3	ALL
F1	92,86%	100,00%	100,00%	97,62%
F2	100,00%	100,00%	100,00%	100,00%
F3	33,33%	33,33%	50,00%	37,50%
F4	50,00%	36,36%	44,44%	43,75%

to the distribution of detection latency with respect to the built-in kernel detection mechanisms. Most of the hangs have been detected *promptly* once the faulty portion of code has been executed (within $1ms$.). However, there is a percentage of failures which have been detected in a long time (up to $1s$.). This is due to the fact that the consistency control code execution may be delayed by the kernel. Furthermore, some detection mechanisms are based on timeouts which can also be very long. Thus, detection latency exhibited by kernel mechanisms cannot be easily predicted. By means of the proposed algorithm, instead, it is allowed to identify an upper bound for the detection latency. This is because hangs are persistent, hence they are eventually detected by the count and threshold mechanism implemented by C. However, latency value depends on the sample period for I/O rate, as well as on the $\overline{C}$ value with respect to the specific workload.

$\overline{C}$ also impacts on detection quality. On the one hand, the greater its value, the better the accuracy (i.e., the lower the number of false positives). Figure 3.5 reports how accuracy depends

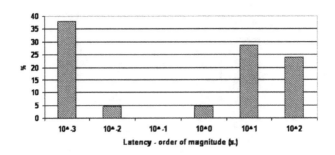

Figure 3.4: Latency distributions of standard logging mechanisms

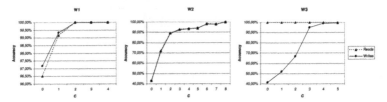

Figure 3.5: Accuracy with respect to the C threshold for each workload

on $\overline{C}$, with respect to each workload. On the other hand, the higher $\overline{C}$, the longer the latency. Hence, a good trade off has to be achieved between detection latency and accuracy. The accuracy follows a similar trend in all workloads (i.e., $accuracy > 90\%$) for $\overline{C} \geq 3$, therefore the algorithm provided good performances for a fixed set of parameters $(\overline{C}, k^+, k^-)$. It is worth noting that $\overline{C}$ has no impact on the coverage (once again due to the persistent nature of KHs). As for overhead, achieved results are summarized in Table 3.3. The two detection mechanisms have been compared both in terms of workload operations per second, and of the amount of data which is read/written to the disks. More in detail, Δ indicates the gap between the two executions of the workloads, and it has been measured with respect to each workload. It can be argued that the overhead does not exceed the 5%, even in the worst case. However, the

Table 3.3: Algorithm overhead

	Ops/s			MB/s		
	Built-in det	Algorithm	Δ	Built-in det	Algorithm	Δ
W1	137,88±30,62	131,66±47,14	-4.51%	0,270±0,064	0,280±0,098	3.70%
W2	818,89±6,11	810,37±5,37	-1.04%	3,389±0,031	3,333±0,047	-1.85%
W3	1901,19±27,56	1880,45±45,99	-1.09%	6,067±0,105	5,990±0,158	-1.27%

difference between averages is always lower than the standard deviation, hence differences are probably due to statistical fluctuations during the experiments. Better results for overhead would have been achieved by using static probing.

3.4.6 Lessons learned

From the above discussed results it can be pointed out that:

1. The detection mechanism provided by the Linux OS reveals some deficiencies which could not be tolerated in mission and safety critical applications, as well as in business critical systems. This confirms the intuition that direct, log-based, techniques are not the best way to perform detection in these systems. The proposed algorithm revealed to provide a better quality, hence it can be effectively used as an additional detection mean.

2. The algorithm has been able to detect kernel hangs, with high quality. Hence, it should be used in the context of a more complex detection system addressing a broader failure model (see section 3.7).

3. Performances of the proposed algorithm are strongly influenced by the tuning, as well as by the running workload.

3.5 Detection system architecture

This section illustrates the general architecture of the detection system, realized to detect application failures, due to software faults, in OTS based complex and critical systems, by leveraging the OS support. Here, the basic principle and ideas are discussed. Its specific application to (i) the detection of application hangs and (ii) the detection of errors in a location oriented perspective, which is the base for the DLR framework, will be described in the next sections. The basic idea is to indirectly inferring the health of the monitored DU by observing its behavior and interactions with the external environment. As stated in section 2.2, OS processes are the target of detection. Hence, since they continuously interact with the external environment (e.g., by means of system calls, signals...), this is particularly effective.

The intuition behind such an approach, which differentiates it from the most of the approaches which have already been proposed, is to leverage OS support to detect upper level failures (e.g., application failures), thus moving down the observation point of view. This way, it is allowed to (i) detect user level failures due to OS faults, and (ii) to have a more complete information set for performing diagnosis.

The overall detection system architecture is depicted in Figure 3.6. It is a modular, pluggable, architecture made up of several OS level monitors (M_i, $\forall i = 1...n$) whose responses, named *alarms*, are combined in order to detect provide a global detection response. This allow to cover a higher number of errors, as well as to gain a better accuracy, if compared to single monitors. Let P the number of $DU s$, i.e., processes, within the monitored application. As monitors are associated to each thread t_j running in the context of the P processes, they account for a total of $P \times t_{jk}$ $\forall k = 1..n$, where n is the number of monitored parameters. The basic idea behind this architecture has been gathered by the anomaly detection paradigm: monitors trigger an alarm if the monitored parameter value deviates from a range of licit values $r_i = [r_i^-, r_i^+]$, which has

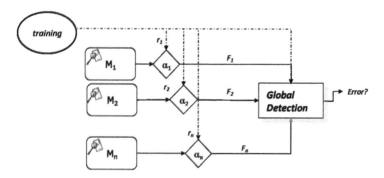

Figure 3.6: Detection architecture.

to be set up during a preliminary training phase. The monitored parameters, and the related ranges, depend on the nature of the application being controlled. More specifically, monitors evaluate a triggering condition periodically, with a period equal to T. An alarm generator (a_i) collects the output of all the monitors related to the parameter n for the $i - th$ process, then it increments a counter, named c, if a given thread verifies the triggering condition. The truth of triggering conditions is established by comparing the values of monitored parameters with those modeled as normal: they are "anomalous" if they fall outside the licit range. In other words, if the monitored value n for a given parameter p does fall outside r_i within a temporal window T, the alarm is triggered. The output of each a_i is thus a variable, named F_i whose definition varies depending on the specific detection strategy (see the following sections).

A similar approach, confirming the intuition that better results could be achieved by combining several monitors, has been proposed in [13], where a model-based approach is followed.

As previously mentioned, this architecture has been used in this thesis (i) for detecting applications hang failures in critical systems and (ii) in the context of the overall DLR framework, where the detection is the crucial input for the location, and then the recovery, of software faults. In particular, the F_i computation, and the global detection function have been specialized to be tailored for the specific case. Details are described in section 3.6 and section 3.7, respectively.

3.5.1 Parameters and detection criteria

The following OS data, which are easy to collect and analyze with a low computational overhead, have been monitored to describe DUs behavior:

1. SIGNALS, i.e., notifications produced by the OS when providing services to the application (e.g., numeric return codes returned by system calls, UNIX signals). Erroneous OS notifications are logged (e.g., return codes different than zero, which represent exceptional conditions and are relatively rare);

2. TIME EVENTS, i.e., the occurrence time of events on which the application relies (e.g., the time in which an OS resource is available to the application, e.g., a semaphore or a network packet). A log entry is produced when timeouts are exceeded, i.e., if such events do not occur within a given interval (e.g., timeout for semaphores availability);

3. THROUGHPUT, i.e., the amount of data exchanged by OS processes through I/O facilities (e.g., the throughput of network and disk devices). Upper and lower bounds are associated with the I/O throughput; throughput is periodically sampled, and a log entry is produced when bounds are exceeded. The detection algorithm, described in section 3.4.4, has been used to monitor these data. It has been slightly improved to pursue this issue, as it will be described in section 3.5.2.3.

3.5.2 The monitors

The detection system has been implemented to be compliant with a POSIX operating system. In particular, we developed it under the Linux OS, and the following monitors have been implemented for controlling the detection parameters $(p = 7)$ described in section 3.5.1.

3.5.2.1 Time related monitors

- *Waiting time on semaphores.* The delay between time in which a task [11] requests for a semaphore and the time the semaphore is actually acquired, for each semaphore and task. An exceeded timeout can be symptom of a deadlock between the threads within a process, or between several processes on the same node.

- *Holding time on semaphores.* The delay between the time in which the task has acquired a semaphore and the time the semaphore is released is measured for each semaphore and task. An exceeded timeout can be due to a process blocked within a critical section.

- *Task schedulation timeout.* The delay between the preemption of a task (e.g., when its time slice is exhausted and the CPU is granted to another task), and the next schedulation of the same task is measured for each task. This way, blocked tasks due to indefinite wait can be detected. For example, the block can be due to a task fault, or to the stall of the overall application (hence, not only to deadlocks).

- *Send/receive timeout on a socket.* The delay between two consecutive packets sent on a given socket (both from and to the monitored task) is measured, for each task and socket. This allows to detect stop and omission failures of a task.

---

[11] A thread in the Linux jargon

3.5.2.2 Signals related monitors

- *UNIX system calls, UNIX signals.* Applications use system calls are to make requests to the OS (e.g., access to hardware devices, process communication, etc.). In UNIX systems, each system call can return a given set of codes which reflect exceptions when the system call exits prematurely. Error codes may be both due to hardware faults and to application misbehaviors (e.g., unavailable file or socket is accessed). Similarly, signals are used by the OS to notify exceptional events which are not related to a system call (e.g., memory denied memory access).

- *Task lifecycle.* The events of allocation and the termination of a task and its descendants are monitored. In fact, when a task terminates, either voluntarily or forcedly, it is deallocated by the OS, and an error code is returned to the parent process; a common rule is to return a non null code in the case of an error.

3.5.2.3 Throughput monitor

This monitor takes into account performance failures which may affect the application. It has been developed by means of an improved version of the algorithm described in section 3.4.4. In fact, when the application is running in degraded mode (e.g., due to resource exhaustion or overloading), it can be observed an anomalous amount of data (either too low, *loss*, or too high, *peak*) produced or consumed by tasks. In order to keep the overhead low, the detection algorithm is very simple and it is based on upper and lower bounds for the I/O transfer rate. Bytes read from and written to disks, and sent to and received from network devices were taken into account. Disk and network operations (both in input and output) within the kernel are probed, and the amount of bytes transferred within a second is periodically sampled (we refer to a sample as $X(t)$). The bounds applied to each metric have to be chosen conservatively (i.e., out-of-bound samples are rare during normal operation), in order to reduce the amount of false positives and still detect the stall of a task. A conceivable way to choose the bounds is to profile the task for a long time period, and to establish the bounds on first-order statistics (i.e., mean and standard deviation) of I/O samples. Different implementations of the algorithm are described in the following sections, with respect to the two cases in which they have been applied. Monitors, which are summarized in Table 3.4, have been implemented by means of *dynamic probing*: the execution flow of the OS is interrupted when specific instructions are executed (similarly to breakpoints in debuggers), and ad-hoc routines are invoked to collect data about the execution (i.e., to analyze OS resource usage by monitored applications). Note that dynamic probing was only used for measurement and detection purposes, and no attempt is made to modify kernel and processes execution. Furthermore, simultaneous failures of the monitors M_i, i.e., the events of producing false alarms at the same time, are assumed to occur rarely. This detection approach reveals to be less intrusive that traditional techniques, such as

Table 3.4: Monitors performing detection.

Monitor	Triggering condition	Parameters	Domain
UNIX system calls	An error code is returned	Window length	Syscalls × ErrCodes
UNIX signals	A signal is received by the task	Window length	Signals
Task scheduling timeout	Timeout exceeded (since the task is preempted)	Timeout value	$[0, \infty]$
Waiting time on semaphores	Timeout exceeded (since the task begins to wait)	Timeout value	$[0, \infty]$
Holding time in critical sections	Timeout exceeded (since the task acquires a lock)	Timeout value	$[0, \infty]$
Task lifecycle	Task allocation or termination	Window length	lifecycle event
I/O throughput	Bound exceeded for C consecutive samples	Threshold C	$[0, \infty]$
Send/receive timeout on a socket	Timeout exceeded (since a packet is sent over a socket)	Timeout value	$[0, \infty]$

those based on heartbeat, which also require extra code to be written at application level, and which may fail in the case of multithreaded applications. Additionally, the proposed approach is able to exploit OS information which would be not available if remote detection were performed: as for example, it allows to discern the nature of a process stuck (i.e., deadlock, I/O waiting...).

3.5.3 Technical Issues

Dynamic probing allows to gather useful information related to system problems in a real environment, e.g., page-manager bugs in the kernel, as well as user or system problems that are not easy to reproduce in either a lab or production environment. As the system as been implemented in the Linux OS environment, the probing has been realized by means of the *Kprobes* framework [12]. It is a simple and lightweight mechanism that enables the insertion of breakpoints into a running kernel. Kprobes provides an interface to break into any kernel routine and collect information from the interrupt handler non-disruptively. It also allows to collect debugging information, such as processor registers and global data structures. More precisely, a probe is inserted by dynamically writing breakpoint instructions at a given address in the running kernel. Execution of the probed instruction results in a breakpoint fault. *Kprobes* hooks into the breakpoint handler and collects debugging information.

When implementing the detection system, breakpoints have been placed in the kernel functions related to the detection parameters. Once the breakpoint is hit, a handler routine is executed just before the kernel code, in order to collect data quickly (e.g., input parameters or return values). This does not introduce any interferences on correct program execution, except for a very short delay.

The complete detection system has been implemented as a loadable kernel module, by means

---

[12]http://sources.redhat.com/systemtap/kprobes/index.html

of the *SystemTap* tool[13]. It allows to program breakpoint handlers by means of a high-level scripting language; *SystemTap* scripts are then translated into C code.

Synchronization issues between threads have been tricky to be monitored. Indeed, tracing the kernel code is not enough for providing a complete view of all the lock/unlock operations on shared resources. For this reason a shared library has been implemented to wrap PThread API provided by the standard *glibc* library which, in fact, overloads the PThread functions to be monitored.

The experienced delays in program executions when using *KProbes* and *SystemTap* have not been significant, i.e., they do not cause sensible overhead. In particular the overall execution time of the application and the time to completion of a single remote method in the absence and in the presence of the detector have been compared . The overall execution time has not been influenced by the detector, since it is mostly dependent on other random factors, such as network delay. As for the time to completion of a single remote method, an average 2.35% overhead due to the detector has been experienced.

3.6 The OS support to detect application hangs

Application hangs can be both active, i.e., hangs that occur when the process is still running (i.e., one of its threads, if any, consumes CPU cycles), but its activity is no longer perceived by other processes and by the user, or passive, i.e., hangs that occur when the process (or one of its threads) is indefinitely blocked, e.g., it waits for shared resources that will never be released. In complex systems it is hard to tell whether a thread is currently subject to a passive hang, or it is deliberately blocked waiting for some work to be performed (e.g., this happens when pools of threads are used in multi-threaded server processes). According to the classification proposed

---

[13]http://sourceware.org/systemtap/

in [15], a given application can fail due to *halt* failures, i.e., failures which cause the delivered service to be halted and the external state of the service to be constant. Crash failures also belong to this class, i.e., a *DUs* is crashed when the process terminates unexpectedly (e.g., due to run-time exceptions). Even if crashes can be considered as the most severe failures, their detection is fairly simple to be performed locally, since the process structure associated with the *DUs* is deallocated when the process crashes. This is the why hang detection is the focus of this part of the thesis. In fact, is it not so simple to detect these failures. By means of preliminary studies conducted on a few safety critical systems, e.g., the CARDAMOM middleware (see Appendix A), it has been shown that they were not so robust to application hangs. In other words, even the middleware built-in logging mechanisms were not able to notify the presence of hangs. This has been confirmed by an experimental campaign aiming to perform a robustness test of the middleware, and of the Fault Tolerance service it provides. Table 3.7 reports a summary of the achieved results, as well as of the experiments setup. It can be argued that the middleware built-in detection mechanisms have been not able to detect the presence of an hang into the server, thus not serving the clients' requests. This is because the server was hang but it was able to respond to the heartbeat anyway.

For this reason a detection system has been realized to support the detection of these failures in complex and safety critical systems. This has been conceived as a self-containing detection system, hence without diagnosis in mind. In this case the following issues have to be pointed out to clarify the specific architecture realization:

1. The specific architecture scheme is depicted in Figure 3.8. An oracle (O) has been used to compare detected failures and the normal behavior of the system. The feedback branch refers to tunable parameters which could be retrained during system lifetime dynamically.

Figure 3.7: Hang failures which escaped the built-in middleware detection mechanisms

Testbed and experiments			
The application workload is a client server application using the CARDAMOM FT service. Three clients invoke the hello() method provided by the server. Server is replicated; if the primary server crashes it should be replaced by the backup replica. Faults have been injected into the code induce application failures. All the hang failures have not been detected by the middleware, i.e., it has not been robust to these failures in that the clients have been not served anymore.			
Test	**Failure**	**Injection location**	**Result**
ServerFailure1	Crash	Callback on _run	Detected
ServerFailure2	Crash	Servant method	Detected
ServerFailure3	Crash	Callback on _run	Detected
ServerFailure4	*Active Hang*	Servant method	*UNDETECTED*
ServerFailure5	*Active Hang*	Servant method	*UNDETECTED*
ServerFailure6	*Passive hang*	Servant method	*UNDETECTED*
HangOverloading1	*Overloading (passive wait)*	Servant method	*UNDETECTED*
HangOverloading2	*Overloading (active wait)*	Servant method	*UNDETECTED*
ServerFailureState1	Crash	State Checkpoint function	Detected
ServerFailureState2	Crash	State Checkpoint function	Detected
ServerFailureState3	*Active Hang*	State Checkpoint function	*UNDETECTED*

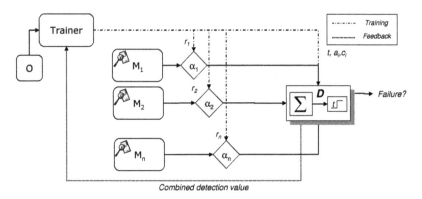

Figure 3.8: Scheme of the detection system

This system is intended for performing failure detection, and it is not going to be integrated with other systems. This is the reason for which the architecture is slightly more complicated than the one depicted in section 3.5. Training and feedback are performed within the system itself; the same holds for the oracle.

2. The output of the global detection, d, has been calculated by means of a weighted sum:

$$d = \sum_{i=1...n} w_i \cdot F_i \tag{3.2}$$

where F_i is defined as:

$$F_i = \begin{cases} -1 & \text{if } n \notin r_i \text{ in T} \\ 1 & \text{otherwise} \end{cases} \tag{3.3}$$

More precisely, let $t(k)$ be the time of the $k-th$ measurement. T(k) is the temporal window containing the measurement, as depicted in Figure 3.9. This windowing technique aims to minimize false positives in the detection process: if the number of times that $n \notin r_i$ within T(k) falls outside r_i, an alarm is signaled. A similar approach is a common in the context of intrusion detection studies, where n-grams are used to extract regular patterns from traces (the number of alarms is used instead of a time interval [77, 79]).

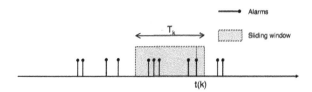

Figure 3.9: Windowing technique to discriminate anomalies

Actual values for each r_i have to be preliminary tuned during the training phase (see the Trainer block in the Figure 3.8). The training is performed by analyzing both normal and faulty runs of the system. It is worth noting that, even in normal executions of the system, anomalous values could appear due to the complexity of the applications we are addressing, e.g., a certain number of threads in a thread pool might be blocked, waiting for being activated; the long waiting time is thus not pathologic in this case. These anomalies are ruled out by the training phase, during which appropriate ranges are established for each monitor.

The weights, w_i, have been assigned to the monitors as in equation 3.4:

$$
w_i = \begin{cases} a_i & \text{if } F_i = 1 \\ c_i & \text{if } F_i = -1 \end{cases}
\tag{3.4}
$$

This allows to take into account monitors detection capabilities: a_i and c_i are respectively the accuracy and the coverage measured for each monitor. Hence, in the weighted sum, positive contributions (each of them equals to a_i) are due to monitors which trigger alarms. On the contrary, negative contributions (each of them equals to c_i) are due to monitors claiming the absence of anomalies. The proposed heuristic is quite simple to calculate, hence it is computationally efficient if compared to data mining or statistical classification techniques.

A failure is finally detected if d in equation 3.2 exceeds a given threshold t. The threshold is set during the training phase in order to be never exceeded during normal runs. Of course, its value can be re-tuned during system lifetime: this justifies the feedback in Figure 3.8. The oracle, O, is responsible for supervising the training and for evaluating a_i and c_i for each M_i and α_i.

3. The socket monitor has not been used in this case, as it was not helpful in this case.

3.6.1 Application hangs detection

The monitor periodically samples the rate of I/O operations, then the computed sample value is compared to the statistical mean. If a given bound is exceeded (see equation 3.5), i.e., if the samples value significantly differs from the average, a given counter, namely C is incremented. On the contrary, if the bound is not exceeded, C is reset to zero.

$$y = \begin{cases} |X(t) - m_X| > k^+\sigma_X & \text{if } X(t) > m_X \\ |X(t) - m_X| > k^-\sigma_X & \text{if } X(t) < m_X \end{cases} \tag{3.5}$$

In the previous equation, $X(t)$ represents the I/O sample at time t, whereas m_X and σ_X represent, respectively, the precomputed mean and standard deviation values. Normal fluctuations around the mean have to be taken into account by properly tuning k^+ and k^-. These thresholds have to be set in order to minimize false positives. For this reason, it is desirable to not have false positives when training the monitor, i.e., during normal executions of the workload (see Figure 3.10a). If this is not achievable (see Figure 3.10b), thresholds have to be set to filter out

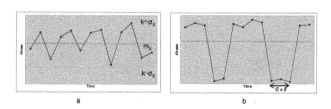

Figure 3.10: I/O operations rate

outliers, i.e., I/O samples which significantly differs from the statistical mean.

The C counter plays a key role in alarm triggering. During normal executions, a threshold value $\overline{C}$ has to be defined which, if exceeded, causes a warning to be triggered. This threshold is introduced to filter short-time deviations from the mean value, which normally occur during workload executions. In order to encompass longer deviations (e.g., long I/O bursts), a more complex model should be defined (e.g., by using Hidden Markov Models to characterize several system states; the same approach can be used on these states with different bounds and $\overline{C}$ thresholds).

3.6.2 Experimental framework

3.6.2.1 Testbed and workload

The case study comes from the real world; it is a CARDAMOM application, exploiting Fault Tolerance and Load Balancing facilities provided by the middleware. The application implements a system in charge of updating flight data plans. Clients forward update requests to a *facade* process, that is replicated by means of CARDAMOM fault tolerance facilities, and which forwards them to several processing servers, configured as a load balancing group. These are in charge of performing perform the actual data plans update; the *facade* collects server responses and informs the clients that the request has been served. Communications between

Figure 3.11: Outcomes of the injection experiments

processes are performed by means of a Data Distribution System (DDS).

The application is deployed on three nodes of a cluster of computers; each node is equipped with a Intel Xeon processor and with 4Gb of RAM memory.

3.6.2.2 Fault injection campaigns

Software Mutation has been used also in this case for injecting faults. The application source code has been corrupted according to the injection framework described in [1]. Faults have been injected both into the facade and one processing server (*pserver* in the following), accounting for a total number of 88 injections (72 faults into the *facade*, the others in the *pserver*). Injected faults resulted in different failures according to the percentages reported in Figure 3.11. "Wrong" means that erratic failures occurred which are not considered in this work. However, they account for the minority of the observed failures. "OK" means instead that the injected fault did not result in a failure.

Results

The approach has been evaluated in terms of accuracy and coverage metrics (see section 3.2). Tunable parameters have been trained empirically. Both timeout values for semaphores waiting times and tasks schedulation have been set to $1s.$, such as the I/O sampling rate and the sliding window length. Results show that the overall approach is robust with respect to sub optimal choices of the tuning parameters; automatic training should be done to set them optimally. Table 3.5 shows accuracy and coverage values for each monitor and with respect to injection target processes (namely *facade* and *pserver*). Performances of single monitors differs significantly. The I/O throughput monitor exhibits better accuracy and coverage for both the processes, if compared to other monitors. Conversely, the holding times on critical sections shows different coverage with respect to the monitored process (0% for the *facade*, and 89.66% for the *pserver*). Hence, it is important to have multiple monitors, since their performance can be influenced by the monitored process. The same set of experiments used for Table 3.5 has

Table 3.5: Coverage and accuracy experienced for each monitor.

Monitor	c_i facade	c_i pserver	a_i facade	a_i pserver
I/O throughput	100%	100%	90.74%	66.67%
Task Schedulation Timeout	83.33%	75.86%	61.11%	57.41%
Waiting times on semaphores	25%	96.55%	77.77%	97.0%
Holding times for critical sections	0%	89.66%	81.48%	90.74%
OS Signals	8.33%	0%	100%	100%
System calls	8.33%	17.24%	97.0%	100%
Processes and threads exit codes	0%	0%	100%	94.44%

been used to set the t threshold (see equation 3.2) for both the processes. It is interesting to note that the threshold values were significantly affected by the monitored process, i.e., it is $t = -468$ for the facade and $t = -195$ for the pserver.

Table 3.6 shows results in terms of accuracy and coverage for the global detection. They (c_{global} and a_{global} respectively) are reported in Table 3.6 and confirm that the combination of multiple monitors improves the overall detection quality. Specifically, the global detection is able to preserve the good coverage result of the I/O throughput monitor, while minimizing the number of false positives, hence improving the overall accuracy. For instance, with reference to the pserver process, using only an I/O throughput-based detector would have led to the same high coverage result. Nevertheless, the accuracy value would have been lower (i.e., $a_i = 66.67\%$) than in the case of the global detector ($a_{global}=100\%$).

This result is achieved despite the empirical training of tunable parameters, which is approximative.

Table 3.6: Global coverage and accuracy

Monitor	c_{global} (facade)	c_{global} (pserver)	a_{global} (facade)	a_{global} (pserver)
Global Detector	100%	100%	96.15%	100%

3.6.3   Lesson learned and possible improvements

The detection of application hangs has been performed with good results by means of the proposed architecture. However, there is still much work to be done in terms of monitors to plug into the scheme, as well as on the global detection heuristic. Of course a good trade off has to be found between performances and computational overhead. Even if the one proposed here exhibits good behavior, further solutions should be investigated, even with respect to different target systems. As a general conclusion, as it will be also confirmed in the next Chapter with respect to the overall DLR framework, the idea of combining multiple detection sources is quite effective. It allows to get the most of each single monitor, thus preserving accuracy and coverage. Finally, the idea of monitoring I/O throughput has been demonstrated to be effective also for detecting application failures, beyond that kernel hangs.

3.7 A novel diagnosis-oriented idea of detection

The idea of integrating detection into the diagnosis process lead to a radical upset of the traditional detection approaches. Their ultimate aim was to optimize detection accuracy, i.e., the percentage of events detected correctly, at design time, in order to let the detectors exhibit the minimum number of false alarms once on the field. This is a very effective approach if a complete, or at least broad, knowledge of the events to detect is available.

When performing error detection in hardware systems, such an hypothesis sounds reasonable, and the approach reveals effective. In fact, these systems can be affected by a restricted number of faults which are easy to detect, and to repair as well (e.g., bit flips or stuck-at-value). Additionally, these faults are likely to have a transient nature (e.g., a sudden temperature peak) hence, if signaled not properly, they could induce unnecessary actions on the system (e.g., the isolation of the component believed as faulty). Thus, they have to be discriminated.

Conversely, when only a reduced set of detectable events is known, a similar approach can be even counterproductive. In fact, it would cause some events to go unnoticed, even being related to faulty conditions. This is especially true in the case of complex software systems, for which the presence of residual faults, mainly Heisenbugs, exacerbates this issue. If they were discriminated, in the same way as hardware transient faults, their consequences could not be tolerated at all. This is what has to be avoided in a recovery oriented diagnosis perspective, such as DLR. *The aim of this section is to propose a novel detection strategy in charge of supporting the location, and then the diagnosis, of software faults in complex and OTS based critical systems.*

Let F be the set of events (faults, errors) which can affect the system. Let it be the union of two subsets:

- K, i.e., the set of events which are known at design time;

- $\overline{K}$, i.e., the set of faults which are not known at design time (potential residual faults, if activated);

Hence, $F = K \cup \overline{K}$. Then, if D is the set of detected events and $\overline{D}$ the set of undetected ones, it holds also that $F \subseteq D \cup \overline{D}$, with respect to detection.

Traditional approaches assume $\overline{K} = \emptyset$, hence detectors were designed so that $\overline{D} = \emptyset$ as well. Thus, their ultimate aim is to keep $K = D$ at design time. In fact, the events in $D - k$ would be false positives.

Conversely, in the case of partial ignorance about the detectable events, it is $\overline{K} \neq \emptyset$, and $\overline{D} \neq \emptyset$ consequently.

In Figure 3.12 the difference between the events encompassed by the detection is depicted. Green triangles in Figure 3.7 correspond to false positives. Known, and actual, faults, that are figured in blue, are always detected to confirm the complete awareness about the events to detect.Figure 3.7, instead, encompasses the presence of both unknown (the red squares) and undetected faults (the crosses). These two classes of events overlap, in that it is not possible to detect something which is not recognized as a known event. In other words, they correspond to false negatives, thus they have to be skilled off. The idea behind the detection strategy proposed in this thesis, is the ability of detect even the presence of unknown events, by keeping in mind the following goals:

- reduce the size of $\overline{K} \cap \overline{D}$ always, i.e., to get maximum coverage;

- reduce the size of $K - D$ over time, i.e., to get an accuracy function increasing with time.

As shown in Figure3.13, this results in a subset of unknown events which are signaled anyway, even if they cannot be completely characterized. A gross grain overview of the overall approach which is proposed in this thesis has been provided in Chapter 2.

As already discussed there, the detection strategy proposed in the context of this work is based on the machine learning paradigm, in the form of anomaly detection. The unknown events which are signaled, are in fact deviations from a system behavior modeled as "normal"; however they could not be related to an actually faulty event.

In section 2.2 the system model and assumptions made in this thesis have been described. According to the terminology used there, the detectable events are in fact "errors" in the state of the system. The OS processes are the object of detection, and location as well (*DUs*).

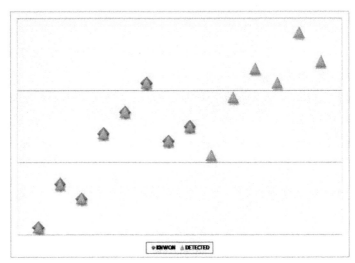

(a) All the events are assumed to be known by traditional detection approaches

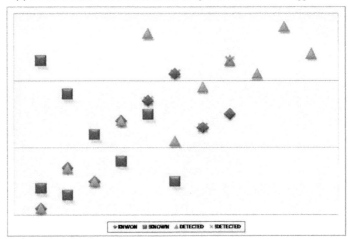

(b) Unknown events come up when transient software faults have to be faced

Figure 3.12: Difference between events in traditional and new approaches for detection.

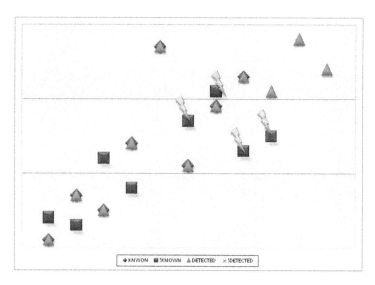

Figure 3.13: Unknown events which go unnoticed

3.7.1 The detection architecture

The detection system designed in this thesis (see section 3.7) to detect application failures, has been slightly modified to be integrated into a diagnosis engine. The following issues have to be pointed out to clarify the changes:

1. The output of each a_i is a binary variable defined as:

$$F_i = \begin{cases} 1 & \text{if } n \notin r_{in} \text{ in T} \\ 0 & \text{otherwise} \end{cases} \tag{3.6}$$

   Ranges r_i are tuned during the training phase; their bounds correspond to the maximum and the minimum number of occurrences of the monitored events (the number of events n is sampled periodically) experienced during faulty-free runs of the system.

2. The global detection response, has been achieved by means of the Bayes' rule. The probability of an error is achieved by:

$$P(F|\underline{a}) = \frac{P(\underline{a}|F)P(F)}{P(\underline{a}|F)P(F) + P(\underline{a}|\neg F)(1 - P(F))} \tag{3.7}$$

   The specialized version of the architecture of the detection system is depicted in Figure3.14. An error is detected, i.e., a detection alarm is triggered, if the estimated *a posteriori* probability exceeds a given threshold. In equation 3.7, F represents the event "faulty DU", and $\underline{a}$ is a vector containing the output of the alarm generators α_i: if $F_i = 1$ for L consecutive periods T, then $\underline{a}_i = L$, in order to take into account the alarm duration and to filter out "transient" false alarms (i.e., alarms triggered for only a short amount of time). The joint probability distributions $P(\underline{a}|F)$ and $P(\underline{a}|\neg F)$, i.e., the probability of detection

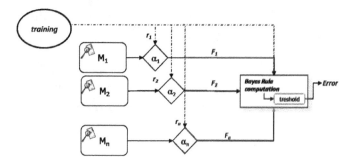

Figure 3.14: Architecture of the location oriented detection system

and the probability of false alarms respectively [86], have to be estimated during the train-ing phase. The former can be estimated using fault injection, by evaluating the number of occurrences of the **a** vector under faults, over the total number of vectors collected during fault injection. Similarly, the latter can be estimated by counting the number of occurrences of **a** during faulty-free executions. Finally, the *a priori* fault probability $P(F)$ has to be known. Field data, if available, or statistical characterization provided by the literature can be used to this aim.

3. All the monitors described in section 3.5.2 have been used.

3.7.2 I/O throughput monitoring for location oriented detection

In this case, the detection algorithm has been formulated as in equation 3.5. It can be formu-lated more clearly as:

$$y = \begin{cases} 1 & \text{if } X(t) > m_X \quad \text{and } |X(t) - m_X| > k^+\sigma_X \\ 1 & \text{if } X(t) < m_X \quad \text{and } |X(t) - m_X| < k^-\sigma_X \\ 0 & otherwise \end{cases} \tag{3.8}$$

were m_X and σ_X are the mean and the standard deviation of the profiled samples during the training phase, k^+ and k^- are constants preliminary set by the user (greater constants will lead to more conservative bounds). In order to take into account bursts and idle periods, a threshold C is chosen such that an error log entry is produced only if C consecutive out-of-bound samples occurs; C can be set to the maximum length of the bursts or idle periods occurred during the training phase.

3.7.3 Experimental campaigns

The effectiveness of the detection approach described in section 3.7 has been evaluated again by means of fault injection campaigns. However, to give the reader on overall picture of the overall DLR framework, and of at what extent the proposed strategy helps the diagnosis of software faults, details about the conducted experiments are delayed to the next chapter (see section 5.5). There, a thorough description of experiments will be provided; both detection and location results will be shown and discussed.

Chapter 4

Fault Location and Recovery

This chapter aims to illustrate the location strategy, in charge of locating the root cause of a failure once an alarm has been triggered by the detection module. It is also able to improve detection accuracy over time, by reducing the number of false positives through periodic feedback actions. The problem has been addressed as a classification problem, and recovery actions tailored for the particular faults that occurred have been associated to each fault class. Details about the machine learning used strategy, and about the adopted classifiers as well are provided.

4.1 The Location Strategy

In a diagnosis framework, the ultimate aim of location is to provide a fault candidate list, i.e., to identify which faults can (potentially) be the cause of the experienced error/failure. Obviously, the shorter the list, the better the location quality. As stated in chapter 2, the location has been addressed in this thesis as a classification problem.

The underlying approach has been gathered by the machine learning community, which provides a generous literature, as stated in section 2.4. In particular, the approach proposed in this thesis is close in spirit to several works focusing on different problems, e.g., works focusing on document classification [87, 88] or aiming to find latent errors in software programs [59].

To the best of author knowledge, similar approaches have not been applied so far to faults diagnosis. Being the proposed approach oriented to system recovery, faults have been associated to the best recovery action in charge of solving the problem experienced by the system. The information related to a fault, have been translated into "features" that have to be processed by the location classifier (see section 4.2.2).

The basic idea is to associate recovery actions to each experienced fault, thus keeping the classifier aware of the most suitable recovery action to start in the case of actual faults. In fact, for each DU in the system, injected faults are added to the training set, if unknown. This is achieved by means of the training phase, which has been described in chapter 2. This way, a base knowledge is built, even by exploiting human insights where they are available (see chapter 2).

Support Vector Machines (SVMs) have been used for performing classification. The high-performance algorithm they rely on, has been commonly used across a wide range of text classification problems, and they reveal to be quite effective for handling large datasets [89].

In this thesis, a variant of the SVM classifier, named MPSVM [1], has been used. It is able to provide a probability output indicating the level of belief related to the performed classification. These output probabilities have been leveraged to properly diagnose Unknown Faults (see section 2.3), as well as to unmask detection of false positives (i.e., Suspected Errors (SEs) in section 2.3). More precisely, a confidence has been introduced, C, which is in fact the maximum of the output probability vector provided by the classifier. A fault is claimed *unknown* if C is less than a given threshold, t. As for SEs, a special class of faults, named "No Fault", has been introduced: if the classifier is confident that a given fault belongs to this class, (i.e., $C \geq t$), a

---

[1]see details in section 4.2.1

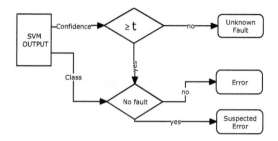

Figure 4.1: Diagnosis response wrt location output

SE is claimed. In this case, the monitor which triggered the alarm is retrained by modifying the joint probability distributions in equation 3.7. In this case, no recovery actions are initiated. The choice of t strongly impacts on the diagnosis quality, hence a sensitivity analysis has been performed for tuning it properly, as it will be detailed in section 5.5.

Figure 4.1 shows the final diagnosis response with respect to the location output.

4.2 Machine Learning

The general problem of machine learning is to search a large space of potential hypotheses to determine the one that will best fit the data and any prior knowledge. Available data can be labeled or unlabeled. In the former case, a supervised learning problem is being faced, in that the true answer is known for a given set of data. A classification problem holds when the output function is a class, i.e., labels are divided into categories. Conversely, if the output is a continuous function, a regression problem arises. In the latter case, instead, labels are unknown and unsupervised learning has to be performed. The main aim is to characterize the structure of the data, e.g. by identifying groups of examples in the data that are collectively similar to each other and distinct from the other data.

In this thesis, the problem of fault location has been faced as a supervised learning problem, in the form of classification. According to supervised learning, some properties have to be predicted, given some examples. If there are available a set of examples whose properties have already been characterized, the task is to learn the relationship between the properties and the collected samples. The approach consists in presenting the examples to a learner which makes a prediction of the property of interest. The correct answer is then presented to the learner that adjusts its hypothesis, accordingly.

In order to solve a supervised learning problem, several steps have to be performed:

1. The nature of the training samples has to be established, with respect to the problem to be solved;

2. A training set has to be gathered, which is representative of real world situations (it may be achieved by field data or human experts into the field);

3. The representation function for the inputs features has to be determined; the better the input objects representation the higher the accuracy of the learned function. Input objects are usually transformed into a feature vector; a good trade off has to be found between the number of features and the prediction accuracy.

4. The structure of the learned function, as well as the learning algorithm to be used (e.g., artificial neural networks or decision trees) have to be established. Then algorithm parameters have to be tuned and validated on a different set of samples (the validation set).

Formally, the goal of the supervised learning is to learn a mapping $h : X \to Y$ from structured inputs to structured response values, where the inputs and response values form a dependency structure. For each input x, there is a set of feasible outputs, $Y(x) \subseteq Y$. It is usually assumed that $Y(x)$ is finite for all $x \in X$, which is the case in many real world problems.

Active learning is a form of supervised learning which is used in the case that there is a lot of unlabeled data which are expensive to be labeled. It is an iterative supervised learning in which the learner queries the trainer for labels. Since the learner chooses the examples, the number of examples to learn a concept will be much lower than the number required in normal supervised learning. Of course, there is a risk that the algorithm might focus on unimportant or even invalid examples.

During each iteration, the set of samples T is broken up into three subsets:

- $T_{K,i}$ i.e., data points where the label is known;

- $T_{U,i}$ i.e., data points where the label is unknown;

- $T_{C,i} \subseteq T_{U,i}$, i.e., a subset of $T_{U,i}$ that is chosen for labeling.

The focus of research is on finding the best method to chose the data points for $T_{C,i} \subseteq T_{U,i}$. Active learning is particularly suitable for solving web searching, e-mail filtering, relevance feedback, and protein recognition problems.

Most active learning algorithms are built upon SVMs, and they exploit SVM structure to determine which data points have to be labeled. Such methods usually calculate the margin, W, of each unlabeled data in $T_{U,i}$; W is a n-dimensional distance from that datum to the separating hyperplane. Datum with the smallest W are those that the SVM is most uncertain about and therefore should be placed in $T_{C,i}$ to be labeled, according to the so-called Minimum Margin Hyperplane methods.

SVMs are statistical classifiers which are adopted with significant success in numerous real-world learning tasks, such as document classification [87], and speech recognition [90]. However, the trickiest issue when performing classification is to select the strategy that is the best for the given problem to get solved. This is because the performance of a given classifier strongly depend on the characteristics of the data to be classified, as well as on the number of features. The main point is that different classification strategies can be compared only by running empirical tests (e.g., the minimization of the empirical risk), which are not always easy to be performed in practice. Besides SVMs, the most widely used classifiers are the Neural Networks (Multilayer Perceptron), k-Nearest Neighbors, Gaussian Mixture Model, Gaussian, Naive Bayes and Decision Trees. Of course each of them is able to solve a given class of problems better than other ones. The following section gives an introduction of SVMs, in order to clarify why they have been used in this thesis for addressing the problem of fault location.

4.2.1 Support Vector Machines

SVM classifiers have been mainly introduced to the aim of solving binary problems, where the class label can take only two different values, and which can be solved by discriminating the decision boundary between the two classes. However, real world problems often require to take more complex decisions, i.e., to discriminate among more than two classes, hence the approach has been extended for handling multi-class problems. Multi Class SVMs (MCSVMs), can be achieved in two ways: (i) by combining several standard, one-class, SVM classifiers (as it is proposed in [91]), and (ii) by formulating a single optimization criteria for the whole set of available data. The basic idea underlying the SVM classification is to find the maximum margin hyperplane which provides the maximum margin among the classes.

Linearly separable problems

Let $\vec{x}_i$ denote the feature vector, and let y_i denote its class label (e.g., $y_i = +1$ if $\vec{x}_i$ corresponds to class A, $y_i = -1$ if $\vec{x}_i$ corresponds to class B). In a linear SVM, a linear decision function is

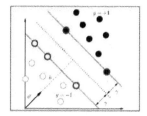

Figure 4.2: SVM representation for linearly separable problems

determined by a unit vector $\vec{w}$ and an offset b as:

$$f(\vec{x}) = sgn(\vec{w}^T\vec{x} - b); \tag{4.1}$$

such that after projecting a data point, $\vec{x}$, onto $\vec{w}$, a positive labeled data will have an output $+1$ while a negative labeled data will have an output -1. The decision function, $f(\bullet)$, is estimated by maximizing γ, subject to the following constraints:

$$\vec{w}^T\vec{x}_i - b \geq \gamma \ \ if \ \ y_i = +1 \tag{4.2}$$

$$\vec{w}^T\vec{x}_i - b \leq -\gamma \ \ if \ \ y_i = -1 \tag{4.3}$$

$$\|\vec{w}\| = 1 \tag{4.4}$$

where γ is the classification margin (dotted line in Figure 4.2). The margin is the minimum distance from a training vector to the decision boundary. The problem consists into finding the $\vec{w}$ and b that maximize the margin (while maintaining linear separability). Constraints in 4.2 force all of the data to be outside the margin region, and $\vec{w}$ to be a unit vector.

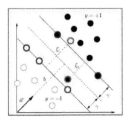

Figure 4.3: SVM representation of non linearly separable problems

Non-linearly separable problems

In the case where the data cannot be separated linearly (Figure 4.3), the optimization problem is adjusted to tolerate some classification errors by means of slack variables, named ψ_i. These refer to each data point $\vec{x}_i$ to indicate its violation from a linear separation. The formulation of constraints becomes:

$$\vec{w}^T \vec{x}_i - b \geq \gamma - \psi_i \; if \; y_i = +1 \tag{4.5}$$

$$\vec{w}^T \vec{x}_i - b \leq -\gamma + \psi_i \; if \; y_i = -1 \tag{4.6}$$

$$\|\vec{w}\| = 1 \; if \; \psi_i \geq 0 \tag{4.7}$$

The overall classification error is given by the sum of the slack variables. The objective function is changed to reflect the compromise between minimizing the classification error and maximizing the classification margin as:

$$max : \gamma - C \sum_{i}^{N} \psi_i \tag{4.8}$$

where $C > 0$ is the penalty on classification errors. For non-linearly separable problems, linear SVM can also be run once the original data have been projected into a certain higher

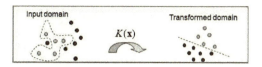

Figure 4.4: Projection of input data in a transformed domain Ω

dimensional Euclidean space, Ω, by means of a kernel function ($K(x)$). The basic idea is to map data to high dimensional space where it is easier to classify them with linear decision surfaces: the problem is reformulated so that data is mapped implicitly to this space. In this case, the problem consists into finding the non linear $K(x)$ function in charge of mapping data into Ω (Figure 4.4). Solving the problem without explicitly mapping the data is desirable, i.e., a $K(x)$ function can be find that does not need to be explicated. This is known as *kernel trick*. As for example, one could take the inner product of projected vectors so that $K(x_i \cdot x_j) = K(x_i) \cdot K(x_j)$, i.e., the image of the inner product of the data is the inner product of the images of the data. Then, data would have not to be explicitly map into the high-dimensional space to solve the optimization problem. Further details about how to classify the projected data can be found in [92].

SVM for multiclass problems

SVMs were originally developed to solve binary classification problems. However, the most of real world problems often require the discrimination between more than two classes. The most popular proposed approaches to solve a $k - class$ problem are:

1. Using k one-to-rest classifiers. This has been demonstrated to be suitable for practical use and consists in constructing and combining k standard SVM classifiers [93];

2. Using k(k-1)/2 pairwise classifiers basing on voting (majority, pairwise coupling);

3. Extending the formulation of SVM to support the $k - class$ problem;

4. Considering all classes at once and then construct the decision function;

5. Construct a decision function for each class by only considering the training data points belonging to that particular class.

A thorough description of all these methods would be out of the scope of this work. The interested reader can refer to [93]. A variant of the SVM multi-class classifier has been used in this thesis, named Multiclass Probability SVM (MPSVM). It is a generalization to the multi-class problem of the Probabilistic SVM classifier (PSVM) proposed by Platt et al. in [94]. The basic idea behind PSVM is to provide calibrated posterior probabilities, informally $P(class|input)$ to enable post-processing, along with the classification output. Standard SVMs do not provide such probabilities. Authors proposed to train an SVM, and then to train the parameters of an additional sigmoid function to map the SVM outputs into probabilities. In formulas, being $\vec{x}_i$ the training samples and $y_i = \{+1, -1\}$ the labels:

$$Pr(y = 1|x) \approx P_{A,B}(f) \equiv \frac{1}{1 + exp(Af + B)} \quad where \ f = f(x) \tag{4.9}$$

Equation 4.9 refers to the binary case. The best parameter setting for A, B is determined by solving a regularized maximum likelihood problem. According to [94], *a posteriori* probabilities are particularly helpful when the classifier is a part of a more complex classifier, or it has to contribute to an overall decision. Since this is quite close to the situation addressed in this thesis, a MPSVM classification scheme has been adopted. Basically, k standard SVM classifiers are combined and single *a posteriori* probabilities are computed by means of the Platt's method (see [94]).

A posteriori probabilities have been interpreted as a *degree of confidence* into the performed classification.

4.2.2 Features for location

In order to train the SVM classifier in charge of performing the location, features have been gathered by several information sources, and at different levels. Basically, middleware and application log files have been processed, as well as OS logs and configuration files.

4.2.2.1 Middleware and application features

In particular, text strings have been extracted with respect to all the executable files in charge of producing logs, as well as with respect to dynamic libraries (e.g. CORBA ORB libraries). Extraction has been performed manually, in a conservative way: all the strings which were likely to be related to error conditions have been included into the feature set (examples of such strings are reported in the leftmost table of Figure 4.5). Then, features have been selected by removing most irrelevant and redundant features from the data, mainly for the sake of dimensionality. This is for enhancing generalization capabilities, as well as for speeding up the learning process. Feature selection has been performed in three steps:

1. Concatenation of all the strings related to a given log (executable files and libraries);

2. Lowercase transformation;

3. Tokenizing, i.e., only a single copy of each token has been considered. This allowed to reduce the number of terms significantly.

The collection of all the achieved token is called *dictionary*. Figure 4.5 shows the process of string tokenizing, i.e., a fragment of the dictionary. Strings refer to the logs generated by the case study application which will be described in the next chapter thoroughly. Beyond log

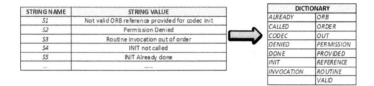

STRING NAME	STRING VALUE
S1	Not valid ORB reference provided for codec init
S2	Permission Denied
S3	Routine invocation out of order
S4	INIT not called
S5	INIT Already done
...	.....

DICTIONARY	
ALREADY	ORB
CALLED	ORDER
CODEC	OUT
DENIED	PERMISSION
DONE	PROVIDED
INIT	REFERENCE
INVOCATION	ROUTINE
	VALID

Figure 4.5: From the collected strings to the dictionary

files, configuration files have been also leveraged as a source of information, and they have been processed in the same way. They reported the name of the host, its IP address, and port numbers used by the running application.

4.2.2.2 Detection Features

Along with logs, also detection alarms have been coded into features in order to trigger the location phase, and to let the location classifier exploit the detection insights. In particular, detection parameters described in section 3.5.1 have been translated in a vector of real elements (which in fact are the features) in order to be exploited by the location classifier. The main goal of these features is to allow the discrimination between false positives and actual faults. Features can be both binary (e.g., they represent the occurrence of an event, like an error of a system call) and real values (e.g., statistics about timeouts within the system, like tasks schedulation times). A list of the detection features is provided in Table 4.1.

4.2.2.3 Features extraction from logs

When a detection alarm is triggered, log files have been processed in two ways: if timestamps were available on the log, the events occurred within the last 3 seconds have been processed; otherwise the last 5 lines of the log have been extracted. These values have been chosen basing on a manual observation of the logs.F

Table 4.1: Features gathered by OS monitors.

Monitor	# of features	Description
UNIX system calls	1141	For each pair (system call, error code), there is a binary feature (it is 1 if the pair occurred, 0 otherwise)
UNIX signals	32	For each signal, there is a binary feature (it is 1 if the signal occurred, 0 otherwise)
Task schedulation timeout	4	Avg, $\sigma(t)$, min, max waiting time for schedulation of DU's tasks
Waiting time on semaphores	4	Avg, $\sigma(t)$, min, max waiting time for a semaphore of DU's tasks
Holding time in critical sections	4	Avg, $\sigma(t)$, min, max holding time for a semaphore of DU's tasks
Task lifecycle	2	Binary features representing the occurrence of tasks newly allocated or deallocated, respectively
I/O throughput	1	Binary feature (it is 1 if the throughput exceeded a bound, 0 otherwise)
Send/receive timeout on a socket	2*4*number of nodes	For each node in the system, Avg, σ, min, max time since last packet sent over sockets to that node, both in input and in output

Avg=mean time; $\sigma(t)$=standard deviation; min/max=minimum/maximum time value

Anyway, the presence of a given token is checked for each extracted entry. If the token is present in the dictionary, the feature value is set to 1, while it is set to 0 if the token is not present. More precisely, it is checked whether a token is in the dictionary or not. For computational efficiency purposes, a hash table has been used to store the dictionary. To conclude, the feature vector is extracted by merging all the vectors extracted from single log files.

4.2.3 Technical Issues

SVM classifier

As for implementation, an open source C library has been used, named *libsvm*[2]. It provides command-line tools to perform training phase (*svmtrain*) and classification (*svm-predict*). Several steps have to be made to properly setup these tools: (i) data conversion in a given format, (ii) data normalization (optional), (iii) SVM classifier selection (OCSVM, MSVM....), (iv) kernel function selection (radial basis function, sigmoidal...), (v) parameter setting, depending on the selected classifier and kernel function. As for data format, target class (i.e., the fault class used to train the classifier) and features have to be listed. Features and values have to be separated by a semicolon ($< feature_i : value >$), and they have to be listed in ascending order. The Radial Basis kernel Function (RBF) has been used in this thesis.

Data management and collection

Data have been collected by the logs by means of Perl scripts. In particular the following functionalities have been developed:

1. Extraction of the log entries related to the alarm (i.e., the last five entries of those related to the last three seconds);

2. Token extraction from log entries;

3. Token search into the dictionary;

In order to compute the global detection output, a centralized script has been used in charge of merging the responses of all the alarm generators. Hence, it has been also necessary to implement the following functionalities:

---

[2]Available at www.csie.ntu.edu.tw/~cjlin/libsvm/

1. Feature vectors transmission to the global detector script by means of a pre-allocated TCP socket;

2. Feature vectors collection;

3. Notification of the "generated alarm" event: all the monitors receive a notification by the detector who generated the alarm in order to let them sending their own responses to the global detector.

Chapter 5

Experimental Results

This chapter illustrates the conducted experiments and the achieved results. A real world middleware
for the development of ATC applications has been used as case study. Experiments show that the im-
plemented diagnosis engine is able to diagnose software faults with good quality and at a low overhead.
Additionally, the aim of reducing detection false positives over time has been accomplished completely.

5.1 A real world case study

The proposed framework has been evaluated on a real world case study, gathered by the Air Traffic Control (ATC) domain. The application has been developed in the framework of an industrial
partnership[1] with Finmeccanica group[2] i.e., the leading Italian Company in the field of mission and
mission and safety critical systems.

The application which has been used as the case study, is a real world application developed to work

---

[1] COSMIC project, http://www.cosmiclab.it
[2] http://www.finmeccanica.com

over an open source middleware platform, named CARDAMOM[3] [95]. This is a middleware for the development of safety critical applications, jointly developed by SELEX-SI[4], a Finmeccanica company, and Thales[5]. These are the two European leaders in the field of ATC, and CARDAMOM is going to be released, its final version, by the end of 2012; it will be installed in the main European airports for air traffic management.

CARDAMOM is a DOM (Distributed Object Model) middleware, based on CORBA and it results from the integration of several OTS items, from libraries to XML parsers, as it is shown in Figure 5.1. It is wrth o note that. CARDAMOM is based on ACE+TAO, i.e., the open source CORBA orb developed by the Vanderbilt University [6], which has been widely used both for academical and industrial research purposes. The presence of third-part modules has been the main reason for which CARDAMOM has been chosen as a case study in the context of this thesis: in fact, it is a real world platform allowing to actually evaluate the impact of OTS items on the overall system dependability, and on the quality of the diagnosis as well. As it is intended for safety critical scenarios, CARDAMOM is able to provide fault tolerance facilities which are compliant with the standard OMG FT CORBA specifications [96]. Further details about the CARDAMOM middleware can be found in Appendix A. The application is part of a complex distributed system, in charge of managing flights' data from the taking off till to the landing phase. Its main goal is to process Flight Data Plans (FPDs), i.e., data coming from Radar Tracks which have to be updated in order to control aircrafts all flight long. The application is also in charge of distributing FDPs to flight controllers, once they have been processed. An overall architectural view of the case study application, is given by the component diagram depicted in Figure 5.2. It encompasses three main components:

- *Facade*, i.e., the interface between the clients (e.g., the Control Working Position, CWP in the ATC jargon, i.e., the flight controller console) and the rest of the system (conforming to the Facade GoF design pattern); it provides a remote object API for the atomic addition, removal,

---

[3]http://cardamom.objectweb.org
[4]http://www.selex-si.com
[5]http://www.thales.com
[6]http://www.theaceorb.com

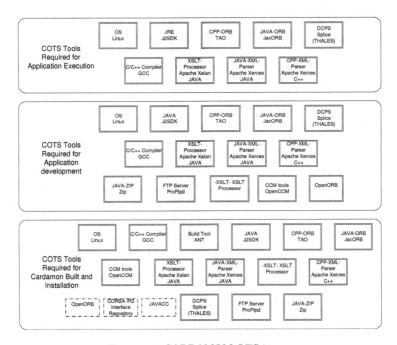

Figure 5.1: CARDAMOM OTS items

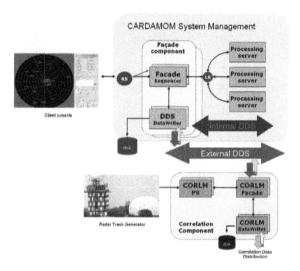

Figure 5.2: Case study architecture.

and update of FDPs. The Facade is replicated according to the warm-passive replication schema. It stores the FDPs along with a lock table for FDPs access serialization;

- *Processing Server* : it is in charge of processing FDPs on demand. It gathers information from the Correlation Component and the FDPs published on the internal DDS. This component is replicated on three nodes, and FDP operations are balanced among servers following a round-robin policy.

- *Correlation component*, which collects flight tracks generated by radars, and associates them to FDPs, by means of Correlation Manager (CORLM in the figure 5.2).

The application workload is in charge of forwarding to the *Facade* the requests coming from the clients; they ask for both flight tracks and FDP updates. To give significance to the workload, requests are made in a random way and at a given average rate.

5.2   Experimental campaign

5.2.1   Objectives

The experimental campaign aimed to accomplish the following objectives:

1. Demonstrate that the detection approach is able to exploit several low-overhead monitors, by keeping low the false positive rate and the detection latency.

2. Demonstrate that the location and recovery modules are able to locate the root cause of a known fault, and to perform the best recovery action respectively. This has to be performed *on-line*, i.e., during system execution, and by exploiting the detection output.

3. Demonstrate the effectiveness of the feedback actions aimed to improve the detection quality over time.

4. Demonstrate the *DLR* capability of capturing unknown events, thus avoiding faults to go unnoticed. This is in order to trigger off-line maintenance (e.g., by alerting human operators) once the system has been put in a safe state by means of the "most severe" recovery action, e.g., a system reboot.

5.3   Evaluation metrics

Detection

As stated in chapter 3, the following quality metrics have been used to evaluate detection approaches (according to [86]):

- *Coverage*, i.e., the conditional probability that, if a fault occurred, it will detected. It is estimated by the ratio between the number of detected faults and the number of injected faults.

- *False positive rate*, which is in fact an accuracy metric, i.e., the conditional probability that an alarm is triggered, given that no actual faults occurred. It is estimated by the ratio between the number of false alarms and the number of normal events monitored.

- *Latency*, i.e., the time between the execution of the fault-injected code, and the time of detection; it is an upper bound for the time between fault activation and the time of detection.

- *Overhead*, which have been estimated by measuring the execution time of remote methods implemented in the Facade remote object; in particular, the execution time for the less and the most costly methods have been evaluated, in terms of execution time (respectively, *update_callback*, and *request_return*).

Location

According to [97, 62], the following metrics have been used to evaluate the location engine:

- *Accuracy*, i.e., the percentage of faults which are classified correctly, with respect to all the activated faults. Letting A and B be two classes of faults, it can be expressed as:

$$A = \frac{TP_A + TP_B}{TP_A + FP_A + TP_B + FP_B} \tag{5.1}$$

- *Precision*, i.e., the conditional probability that, if a fault is classified as belonging to class A, the decision is correct. This metric refers a single class (e.g., A), hence it can be expressed as:

$$P = \frac{TP_A}{TP_A + FP_A} \tag{5.2}$$

- *Recall*, i.e., the conditional probability that, if a fault belongs to class A, the classifiers decides for A. This metric refers a single class too, hence it can be expressed as:

$$R = \frac{TP_A}{TP_A + FN_A} \tag{5.3}$$

In equations 5.2 and 5.3, the quantities TP_A, FP_A and FN_A represent, respectively, the number of True Positives (i.e., the samples of A are classified as belonging to A), False Positives (i.e., the samples not of A are classified as A), and False Negatives (i.e., the samples of A are not classified as A).

5.4 Faultload

The faultload, i.e., the set of faults to inject into application source code, has been designed basing on the field data study conducted by Madeira et al. [1]. Here, additional classes of software faults are encompassed which extend the ODC classification (see section 1.2.4).

In particular, SM has been used to inject faults into the *Facade* and into the *Processing Servers* processes. This has been done by means of the most common fault operators; injected faults are summarized in Table 5.1. Table 5.3 gives more detailed examples of injected faults. The injected

Table 5.1: Source-code faults injected in the case study application.

ODC DEFECT	FAULT NATURE	FAULT TYPE	#
Assignment (63.89%)	MISSING	MVIV - Missing Variable Initial. using a Value	8
		MVAV - Missing Variable Assign. using a Value	5
		MVAE - Missing Variable Assign. using a Value	5
	WRONG	MVAV - Wrong Value Assigned to Variable	26
	EXTRANEOUS	EVAV - Extraneous Variable Assignment using another Variable	2
Checking (6.94%)	MISSING	MIA - Missing IF construct Around statement	2
	WRONG	WLEC - Wrong logical expr. used as branch condition	3
Interface (4.17%)	MISSING	MLPA - Missing small and Localized Part of the Algorithm	2
	WRONG	WPFV - Wrong variable used in Parameter of Function Call	1
Algorithm (20.83%)	MISSING	MFC - Missing Function Call	13
		MIEB - Missing If construct plus statement plus Else...	1
		MIFS - Missing IF construct plus Statement	1
Function (4.17%)	MISSING	MFCT - Missing Functionality	2
	WRONG	WALL - Wrong Algorithm (Large modifications)	1
Total			72

faults listed in Table 5.1 are representative of the most common mistakes made by developers. In the ODC perspective, faults are characterized by the change in the code by which they can be fixed. Faults operators in [1] describe the rules to locate representative fault locations within source code. The most common way for selecting the components where faults have to be injected, is to take into

Fault Class(es)	Description	Example of possible causes	Portion of code(sw)
Assign.	Wrong Value Assigned to Variable	Wrong output from another function. Lack of attention	#if defined(SFI_WVAV_FACADE_001)//Wrong Value Assigned to Variable char* codes[10] = {"abc", "def"}; #else char* codes[10] = {"abc", "def"};
	Extraneous Variable assignment using another Variable	Unfriendly variables naming. Lack of attention	#if defined(SFI_EVAV_FACADE_001) id_temp=d_temp; #else id_temp=d_temp=c_temp; #endif
	Missing Variable Initialization using a Value	Initialization dependent of execution path	#if defined(SFI_MUIV_FACADE_001) #else p.mutex = new Comiv::DsSupport::Mutex::Mutex(); #endif
Check.	Missing IF construct Around statement	IF(x==0) instead of IF(a==0)	#if defined(SFI_MIA_F6_001) #else if(data_sen.length()>0) #endif
	Wrong logical expression used as branch condition	Lack of attention	#if defined(SFI_WLEC_FACADE_001) if(rN0rM==0){ #else if(rN0rM==0){ #endif
Interf.	Missing small and Localized Part of the Algorithm	Non-trivial execution paths inside functions	#if defined(SFI_MLPA_FACADE_001) state[(index*DIM)]=s; state[(index*DIM)+1]=c; state[(index*DIM)+2]=c; #else state[(index*DIM)]=s; state[(index*DIM)+1]=c; state[(index*DIM)+2]=s; #endif
	Wrong variable used in Parameter of Function Call	Func(x,y) instead of func(y,x) with x and y of compatible data type	#elif defined(SFI_WPFV_FACADE_001) save_state(index,fdprid) #else save_state(index,client_back) #endif
Algor.	Missing IF construct plus statement plus Else Before statement	Bad indenting pratice plus single statement mixed with multiple-statement	#if defined(SFI_MIEB_FACADE_001) c_temp=state[i]; id_temp=d_temp=c_temp; #else if(i!=0){ locks[i].flag=flag_temp; j++; }else{ c_temp=state[i]; id_temp=d_temp=c_temp; lock[i].flag=flag_temp; }
	Missing Function Call	Typo: Lack of attention	#if defined(SFI_MFC_FACADE_007) #else int index=block(fdprid);
	Missing IF construct plus Statement	Usage of complex expression such as (a==b && c==d || d==e)	#if defined(SFI_MIFS_FACADE_001) #else if(i!=0){ lock[i].flag=flag_temp; locks[i].client_back_id=CORBA::string_dup(id_temp.c_str()); j++; }
Function	Missing Functionality	Lack of attention	#if defined(SFI_MALL_FACADE_001) COUT_TIMESTAMP("FAULT") ... if(lock[i].id==fdprid){ index=i; i=lock.size(); exist=true; } if (exist==false) index=-1; #else if(locks[i].id==fdprid){ index=i; i=lock.size(); exist=true; } ... if (exist==false) index=-1; #endif

Figure 5.3: Examples of faults actually injected into the facade.

```
/*————————————————SOFTWARE FAULT INJECTION————————————————*/

#if defined(SFI_WVAV_FACADE_001)//Wrong Value Assigned to Variable   COUT_TIMESTAMP("FAULT!")
   char* codes[10] = { "abc", "defg", "ghi", "jkl", "mno", "pqr", "stu", "vwx", "yza", "bcd" };
#elif defined(SFI_WVAV_FACADE_002)
   COUT_TIMESTAMP("FAULT!")
      char* codes[10] = { "abc", "de", "ghi", "jkl", "mno", "pqr", "stu", "vwx", "yza", "bcd" };
#elif defined(SFI_WVAV_FACADE_003)
   COUT_TIMESTAMP("FAULT!")
      char* codes[10] = { "abc", "", "ghi", "jkl", "mno", "pqr", "stu", "vwx", "yza", "bcd" };
#elif defined(SFI_WVAV_FACADE_004)
   COUT_TIMESTAMP("FAULT!")
      char* codes[10] = { "abc", "123", "ghi", "jkl", "mno", "pqr", "stu", "vwx", "yza", "bcd" };
#elif defined(SFI_WVAV_FACADE_024)
   COUT_TIMESTAMP("FAULT!")
      char* codes[10] = { "abcde", "def", "ghi", "jklmn", "mno", "pqruv", "stu", "vwx", "yza", "bcd" };
#elif defined(SFI_WVAV_FACADE_025)
   COUT_TIMESTAMP("FAULT!")
      char* codes[10] = { "ab", "def", "ghi", "jklmn", "mn", "pqru", "stu", "vwx", "yzat", "bc" };
#else
   char* codes[10] = { "abc", "def", "ghi", "jkl", "mno", "pqr", "stu", "vwx", "yza", "bcd" };
#endif
/*————————————————————————————————————————————————————————*/
```

Figure 5.4: *SM*. Faults have been injected into the code via conditional compiling

account software complexity metrics: the more complex the software, the higher the probability of residual faults [98]. By analyzing the application source code, it has been argued that the Facade and Processing Server remote objects (C++ classes) have the major complexity in terms of Lines Of Code (LOCs) and cyclomatic complexity. For this reason, faults have been injected in these classes accounting for a total number of 72 (56 for the Facede and 16 for the Processing Server classes). In practice, injection has been realized by means of conditional compiling directives; a fragment of the code implementing injection is shown in Figure 5.4. This way, faults have injected one per program execution and they are never activated simultaneously. This means that the simultaneous occurrence of more than one fault is not encompassed in this experimental campaign. The fault set has been divided into two subsets of the same size; samples to each subset have been assigned randomly. The former subset, named *training set*, has been used to train and setup the detection and location modules; the latter, also called *testset*, has been used to test the effectiveness of the two phases, and of the overall *DLR* framework as well.

The testbed

Experiments have been run on the 128 nodes computer cluster provided by the Laboratorio CINI-ITEM "Carlo Savy", where the entire research work described in this thesis has been conducted. The case study application has been deployed on 9 nodes (two Facade replicas, one for the CARDAMOM Fault tolerance service, one for Load Balancing Service, three for the FDP processing servers, and 2 nodes are allocated to the Client and to CORLM component, respectively) wired by Gigabit LAN. For the sake of results reliability, and to exclude biasing due to hardware errors, the cluster has been partitioned in 10 LANs: experiments have been executed on the 10 partitions, simultaneously. Global results have been achieved by filtering and averaging the results obtained on each single network. Nodes hardware equipment consisted of 2 Xeon Hyper-Threaded 2.8GHz CPUs, 3.6GB of physical memory, and a Gigabit Ethernet interface; nodes are interconnected through a 56 Gbps network switch.

5.5 Experiments and results

This section provides details about the processed log files, the selected features, and the fault classes. Error messages have been extracted by processing both binary files and libraries of the application, as well as of the OTS libraries (e.g., CARDAMOM, TAO). The *strings* UNIX utility has been used to this aim. The number of collected error messages has been significant, more than 7000, as well as the number of keywords included into the dictionary, which was about 6000. As for features, they account for a total of 17171, taking into account all the running *DUs*. Details are summarized in Table 5.2.

Classes have been associated to each fault, once all the injection experiments have been executed preliminarily. Several failure modes have been observed, i.e., faults surfaced in different failures. A recovery mean (the best one) and a root cause have been associated to each class, as summarized in Table 5.3.

Table 5.2: Diagnosis features details

Number of logs file types	8
Number of monitored log files	16
Number of OTS libraries	87
Number of log messages	7691
Number of extracted tokens within log messages	6043
Number of application keywords	33
Monitored processes by the OS	Facade, 3 Servers
Number of OS features (per process)	1250
Total amount of features	17171

Table 5.3: Fault classes and association with recovery means.

FAULT CLASS	TYPE	LOCATION	RECOVERY
Class 0	No fault	None	The system is correctly working.
Class 1	Crash	Facade	Activate the backup replica; a new backup replica is activated.
Class 2	Passive hang	Facade	Locked resources free and preempted transaction kill. The success of the recovery depends on application properties (e.g., the FDP will be correctly updated by the next update operation);
Class 3	Crash	Server	Reboot the server process, add it to the load balanced group.
Class 4	Passive hang (at start time)	Facade	Application reboot. The application might have failed due to transient faults, then the reboot may succeed on the second try. Human intervention may be required if the reboot does not succeed.

5.5.1 Detection

The detection system described in chapter 4 has been integrated into the DLR framework to support the location phase. This section aims to describe results related to the detection with respect to the application case study, as well as to discuss the effectiveness of the proposed mechanism. First of all, the performance of individual monitors have been evaluated. This is in order to (i) evaluate the effectiveness of single monitors and (ii) to quantify the benefits of the global detection approach. For each monitor, a sensitivity analysis has been conducted: parameter's value of the target monitor have been let vary within the range $[1s, 4s]$ (see table 3.4). The best values gathered by the sensitivity analysis, with respect to the Facade and Server DUs respectively, are shown in Table 5.4 and in

Table 5.5. Different monitors achieve different performances in terms of coverage, since they are suited for different failure modes; actually, monitors are unable to achieve full coverage, except for the *SOCKET* monitor. Furthermore, performances vary with respect to the considered *DU*. As for example, in the case of the Processing Server, only crashes (class 3 in Table 5.3) have been observed, hence no faults have been identified by the monitors devoted to the control of blocking conditions (e.g., wait for a semaphore). All the monitors experienced the same mean latency as they have been triggered together right after the abortion of the *DU*.

The most of the monitors provided a reasonable percentage of false positives. However, there are some for which the rate of False Positives (FP) has been very high (e.g., the UNIX system call monitor triggered the 36.08% of false positives over all the triggered alarms). It is crucial to filter out false positives in order to allow monitors to be included into the system and to bring benefits to the overall detection engine. This increases the amount of covered faults, and hence the overall coverage, and it allows to better support the location phase.

Table 5.4: Coverage, FP rate, and latency provided by the monitors. (Facade *DU*)

Monitor	Parameter value	Coverage	FP rate	Mean Latency ($ms.$)
UNIX semaphores hold timeout	4 s	64.5%	36.08%	1965.65
UNIX semaphores wait timeout	2 s	67.7%	1.7%	521.18
Pthread mutexes hold timeout	4 s	64.5%	4.01%	469.51
Pthread mutexes wait timeout	-	0%	0%	-
Schedulation threshold	4 s	74.1%	3.25%	1912.22
Syscall error codes	1 s	45.1%	0.6%	768.97
Process exit	1 s	45.1%	0%	830.64
Signals	1 s	45.1%	0%	816.57
Task lifecycle	1 s	35.4%	0.05%	375.7
I/O throughput network input	3 s	77.3%	0.4%	4476.67
I/O throughput network output	3 s	77.3%	0.2%	2986.4
I/O throughput disk reads	3 s	70.9%	0.4%	4930
I/O throughput disk writes	2 s	67.6%	0.05%	6168.57
Sockets	4 s	100%	3.47%	469.58

Table 5.5: Coverage, FP rate, and latency provided by the monitors. (Server DU)

Monitor	Parameter value	Coverage	FP rate	Mean Latency ($ms.$)
UNIX semaphores hold timeout	2 s	0%	3.61%	-
UNIX semaphores wait timeout	2 s	0%	2.28%	-
Pthread mutex hold timeout	2 s	0%	4.44%	-
Pthread mutex wait timeout	-	0%	0%	-
Schedulation threshold	1 s	0%	3.25%	-
Syscall error codes	1 s	100%	0.98%	522.5
Process exit	1 s	100%	0.005%	522.5
Signals	1 s	100%	0.005%	522.5
Task lifecycle	1 s	100%	0.22%	522.5
I/O throughput network input	3 s	100%	0.49%	522.5
I/O throughput network output	3 s	100%	87.35%	522.5
I/O throughput disk reads	3 s	100%	79.31%	522.5
I/O throughput disk writes	3 s	100%	77.77%	522.5
Sockets	2 s	100%	3.14%	522.5

Results shown in Table 5.6 are related to the global detection system. The detector is able to achieve full coverage, i.e., all the injected faults did result in errors which have been detected. Additionally, the FP rate has been kept low, in that it never exceeds the 7%: in other words, the global detection accuracy has been increased significantly if compared to that of single monitors. The achieved values are comparable to the best ones experienced by single monitors, for both the monitored DUs. To have a gross grain estimate of the benefits, the average FP rate of the monitors has been calculated: if the global detection algorithm would have not been used, they would have exibithed a FP rate equal to 6,87% and 18.23% for the Facade and the Processing Server DUs respectively. Hence, with respect to results in Table 5.6, FP rate has been lowered of the 1,02% and of the 12,37% for the two monitored DUs.

Last, but equally relevant, better results have been achieved with respect to the latency too.

Table 5.6: Coverage, accuracy, and latency experienced by the global detection system.

	Facade	Server
Coverage	100%	100%
False positive rate	4.85%	6.86%
Mean Latency	100.26 ± 135.76 ms	165.67 ± 122.43 ms

Overhead

In order to estimate the overhead of the detection system, i.e., how much it interferes with the workload execution, the execution times of the two most frequently invoked methods (i.e., FDP update and request callbacks) have been measured. This has been done by letting the client requests rate vary. First, the execution times have been measured when the detector was not running. Then, these have been compared with the execution times experienced when the detector was activated. As it is shown in Figure 5.5 and Figure 5.6 the overhead never exceeded the 10%, even in the worst case , i.e., during the most intensive workload periods.

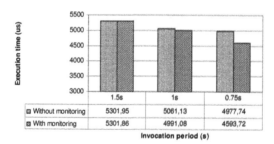

Figure 5.5: Overhead(Facade *update_callback()* method).

5.5.2 Location

Location has been evaluated with respect to both known and unknown faults. The former correspond to faults which have been submitted to the diagnosis engine during the training phase. With respect to

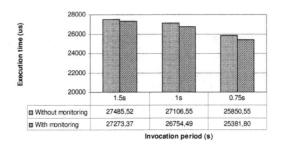

Figure 5.6: Overhead (Facade *request_return()*method.

them, classification capabilities have been evaluated. The latter, instead, correspond to faults which were never submitted to the engine before. In fact, they are faults which resulted in unexpected failures. In particular, the faults labeled as belonging to "Class 4" have been counted out during the training phase. First, location performances have been evaluated with respect to the remaining classes (from Class 0 to Class 3), with a low confidence level ($C = 0.9$). In this case, the location classifier has been always able to classify the fault correctly. Furthermore, it has been able to catch all the false positives coming from the detection system, as shown in Table 5.7. The Table refers to the case where samples of all the classes have been included into the training set. Then, "Class 4" entries have

Table 5.7: Location accuracy wrt to the confidence level

Confidence	Accuracy
0.9	100%
0.99	94.29%
0.995	94.29%
0.999	71.43%
0.9999	25.71%

been submitted to the location classifier. Achieved results are summarized in Table 5.8. As it can be argued by the above results, coverage is far from meeting the requirements of a critical system, at least when the confidence level is $C = 0.9$. In this case, known faults have been classified correctly but, despite of this, only the 5% of the unknown faults have been catched correctly. This means that

Table 5.8: Location performances in the presence of unknown faults (class 4)

Confidence	ACCURACY	P(KNOWN)	R(KNOWN)	P(UNKNOWN)	R(UNKNOWN)
0.9	60%	59.09%	100%	100%	5.26%
0.99	75.56%	70.27%	100%	100%	42.11%
0.995	77.78%	73.52%	96.15%	90.91%	52.63%
0.999	75.56%	80%	76.92%	70%	73.68%
0.9999	42.22%	n.a.	0%	42.22%	100%

the most of them have been misclassified, or even worse, they went unnoticed.

In order to understand the reason for so poor results, the impact of confidence level, which was likely to be low for pinpointing unknown entries, has been further investigated . Results of such a sensitivity analysis are reported in Table 5.8.

Note that the higher the confidence level, the lower the coverage with respect to known faults (i.e., the number of the known faults which is classified correctly, decreases). Hence, a trade off has to be looked for when tuning the engine. For the application case study, confidence levels equal to $C = 0.99$ and $C = 0.995$ allow to classify known fault correctly, and to identify a high number of unknown faults as well (42.11% and 52.63% respectively). Hence, the objective of the tuning phase is to keep the recall as much as possible next to 1, with respect to the unknown faults.

The location of a faults encompasses two temporal contributions. The former is the time required for collecting data by the detection system, once an alarm has been triggered. The latter is the time required for performing actual classification and location of the fault. Table 5.9 shows the results which have been achieved with respect to the conducted experimental campaign. It is shown that the overall location takes less than $1.2s$. on average. This can be interpreted only with respect to system requirements. For a safety critical system, it could be a good results. For hard real time systems, as for example, it could be an unacceptably long time. However, the presence of OTS items contributes to make the location, and diagnosis process as well, longer than one could expect. Better results would have been achieved for more specialized and bespoke, ad-hoc, systems. The last significant result which is worth discussing, concerns the actual capability of the location phase to improve the

Table 5.9: Location times

Mean time for data collection	84.4 ± 115.11 ms
Mean time for location	917.14 ± 23.63 ms

detection quality over time. In order to demonstrate this point, the false positive rate exhibited by the detection system has been monitored during all the experiments. As it is shown in Figure 5.7, a significant amount of false positives has been experienced at the beginning of workload execution. In fact, up to about 250 false alarms have been triggered during the first hour of execution. Then, the retraining action performed by the location phase pursued its aim: the number of false positives dramatically decreased, till being equal to zero.

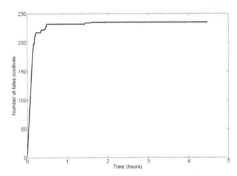

Figure 5.7: Cumulative number of false positives over time.

Conclusions

This dissertation addressed the problem of software faults diagnosis in complex, OTS based, critical systems. The problem has not been solved so far, mainly due to the presence of software faults which can manifest transiently thus making quite difficult to reproduce the conditions for their activation, which depend on environmental factors. These faults, which become even more tricky to face in the presence of OTS items, advocate the need for a recovery oriented diagnosis approach which is the key for achieving fault tolerance.

This dissertation proposed a *holistic approach which encompasses the phases of detection, location, and recovery*. This represents a novel contribution, in that these phases have never been integrated before to perform fault diagnosis in OTS based e legacy systems. First, detection has almost always been considered as a separate task, and its impact on the diagnosis of faults has been underestimated. Second, recovery has been performed manually, rather than automatically, thus requiring human involvement and long downtimes in many cases.

The proposed framework has been named *DLR* to explicitly recall the phases of *D*etection, *L*ocation and *R*ecovery. An engine implementing this framework has been developed which has been evaluated on a real world safety critical system, intended for the development of Air Traffic Control applications. The system has been implemented to run in Linux environment, although the proposed approach, as well as the designed architecture, are general enough to be used in several scenarios and on different systems.

The most significant research contributions brought by this thesis are:

- The intuition that detection has to be integrated into the diagnosis process to encompass transient software faults. This is novel in that this has been stated in [60] theoretically but no actual implementations of such an integration have been made so far;

- The exploitation of OS support to detect application failures. This is novel in that the most common detection techniques are direct, i.e., they observe the system directly by means of logs produced by the monitored entities, or by monitors implemented within the controlled system.

- The ability of detecting, and then repairing, even a subset of faults which is "unknown", i.e., faults which never occurred before. This is a novel contribution in that all the previous approaches did not encompass the presence of these faults (which are in fact the cause of field failures) i.e., they assumed the fault model to be completely known at design time. Run time falls, in fact, were ignored completely, thus they were likely to result in false negatives. Obviously, this is not acceptable in safety and mission critical scenarios.

To corroborate these intuitions, the thesis demonstrated that:

1. sometimes built-in middleware detection mechanisms are unable to detect hang failures by their own (section 3.6);

2. the most of application hang failures can be detected by means of OS level detectors (section 3.4.5).

The self-detection capabilities of the Linux kernel have been investigated in order to quantify their trustworthiness. Some deficiencies emerged when detecting kernel hangs, hence a detection algorithm has been implemented to support kernel hang detection (coverage has been improved of 25%). Then, a complex detection architecture has been designed to detect (i) application hangs and (ii), to detect application failures in a location oriented perspective. The architecture is modular, and it is based on several monitors whose responses are combined to provide a global detection output. In both the cases, the kernel hang detection algorithm has been used as one of the monitors. Results demonstrated the effectiveness of the proposed detection approach, which has been achieved at a low overhead (less than the 5% in all the experimental setups). Overall, the results demonstrated that:

1. The detection approach is able to exploit several low-overhead and inaccurate monitors at the OS level, by keeping low the false positive rate and the detection latency as well;

2. The proposed location and recovery strategies are able to correctly locate the root cause of a known fault within the system, and to trigger the proper recovery action in an on-line manner. Known faults have been covered completely, with both a precision and recall equal to 1 (section 5.5.2)

3. The implemented DLR framework is able to partially discover unknown faults within the system. This is useful to trigger off-line maintenance (e.g., by alerting a human operator). In particular, the DLR engine has been able to detect up to the xx% of unknown injected faults, without compromising the detection of known faults, which have been detected with a 100% coverage.

4. The machine learning approach has been helpful for reducing the number of false positives triggered by the detection over time, by means of the feedback actions triggered by the location module (section 5.5.2).

Appendix A

CARDAMOM

CARDAMOM is a middleware platform enabling component based software architecture for the implementation of safety and mission critical systems, such as those for air traffic control and combat management systems. It has been jointly developed by SELEX-SI and THALES, i.e., the two European leaders in these fields.

CARDAMOM provides a framework for the integration of both Business Components of the functional architecture and Technical Components of non-functional architecture. Components are either proprietary components or COTS (Commercial Off The Shelf) components. CARDAMOM is based on the main interoperability standards, defined by the Object Management Group (OMG) organization:

- UML (OMG standard) and XML (W3C standard) at business level;

- CCM OMG standard in order to separate the business logic from the technical services;

- CORBA OMG standard at technical level.

The major principles on which it relies on are:

- CARDAMOM is multi-domain, as it is intended to be used by different Units in several domains such as Air Traffic Control, Naval Combat Management, Electronic Warfare, Airborne Command, and Control systems;

- Distribution and promotion of CARDAMOM as an Open Source product, in order to allow a wide use of the product and thus to ensure its reliability, durability and long-term support;

- CARDAMOM is CORBA-based. CORBA has been selected as it is a non-proprietary middleware standardized by the OMG and it actually supports heterogeneity across hardware platforms and programming languages, thus is suitable to integrate smoothly legacy systems. CARDAMOM also supports the CORBA Component Model (CCM) which allows to make a clear separation between the functional properties (application logic) and the non-functional properties (technical services).

- Support of the CORBA Fault Tolerance, as well as the provision of mechanisms allowing to develop fault-tolerant applications as well as a fault-tolerant middleware platform (with no single point of failure). CARDAMOM provides the WARM-Passive replication style, and the appropriate fault-tolerance mechanisms allowing managing transparently failure detection, request retry and redirection. In terms of consistency, it provides the State Transfer Framework (DataStore API) facility which assures strong replica consistency.

A.1 CARDAMOM Services

As shown in Figure A.1, CARDAMOM provides two classes of services: basic and pluggable. The former are mandatory and thus are always included in a user application. Other CARDAMOM services rely on them services to pursue their mission.The latter, instead, are optional hence a user application can use only the services it needs as they are independent one on the other.

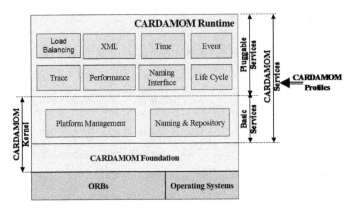

Figure A.1: Services provided by CARDAMOM

Services can be implemented as separate processes (i.e. that do not include application software) or as libraries. In the first case, their are selected at system level: depending on whether a service is needed or not, a CARDAMOM-based system will include or not the corresponding process(es). In the second case, service selection is performed on a per process basis: every process can choose the subset of services it wants to use. The most used services are listed and described shortly in the following.

- *System Management.* This service supports the system technical supervision allowing to handle and monitor the elements (systems, nodes, application, processes, components, group of fault tolerant or load balanced items) making up a system. It covers the initial definition of the system configuration as well as its modification during system operation. Additionally it is responsible for the control of system elements (initialization, start, stop, switch-over, initialization order and the termination order of application software), and of user-defined objects lifecycle. It is in charge of performing system monitoring, including the detection of faulty elements and the monitoring of node resources (CPU load, memory occupation). System reconfiguration to cope with faults and thus to ensure the continuity of system operation despite failures is also responsibility of this service. Finally, it provides notification to subscribers (application software, administration tools) about status and configuration changes of managed elements, including filtering capabilities in order to reduce the amount of information exchanged. System Management modules that could have been single points of failures are replicated.

- *Life Cycle service*, which provides a framework for creating and deleting CORBA objects and managing servants life cycle through pre-defined strategies; it is accessible through an interface providing location and access transparency. It allows to use the POA easily, allowing the selection of POA advanced features.

- *Repository service*, which provides a scalable object repository to store and retrieve object references and attributes. This service provides CORBA Naming and Property Services compatible interfaces and an access independent from programming languages.

- *Event service*, which supports asynchronous communication (using push model and generic event channel) and provides add-on software encapsulation ORB implementation specific features such as event channel creation and that eases connection to event channels.

- *Data Distribution*, which supports the creation and the synchronization of replicated data pools stored on the local memories of different hosts. Based on a Publish-Subscribe model, it allows the asynchronous updates to the local data pools and the possibility of finding the current state of the data pool when connecting for the first time, or when reconnecting after an absence. It complies with the OMG Data Distribution Service (DDS).

- *Time Management*, which provides (i) multiple views of time based on clock characteristics such as resolution, precision, time scale and (ii), timed execution of an operation after a user-specified delay. IT complies with the OMG "Enhanced View of Time" service.

- *Load balancing*, which is responsible to dynamically dispatch client requests across available servers, in order to optimize response times and resource usage according to several policies. The Load Balancing infrastructure is replicated so as not to be a single point of failure.

- *Traces and Performance service* allowing the run-time analysis of middleware platform as well as application software, by providing traces that can be enabled, disabled, or filtered at runtime and stored on disk. It includes several selection criteria that can be set at runtime so as to provide only information in which users are interested.

Bibliography

[1] J.A. Duraes and H.S. Madeira. Emulation of software faults: A field data study and a practical approach. *Software Engineering, IEEE Transactions on*, 32(11):849–867, Nov. 2006.

[2] Marco Serafini, Andrea Bondavalli, and Neeraj Suri. Online diagnosis and recovery: On the choice and impact of tuning parameters. *IEEE Trans. Dependable Secur. Comput.*, 4(4):295–312, 2007.

[3] Alessandro Daidone, Felicita Di Giandomenico, Andrea Bondavalli, and Silvano Chiaradonna. Hidden markov models as a support for diagnosis: Formalization of the problem and synthesis of the solution. In *SRDS '06: Proceedings of the 25th IEEE Symposium on Reliable Distributed Systems*, pages 245–256. IEEE Computer Society, 2006.

[4] Silvano Chiaradonna, Domenico Cotroneo, and Luigi Romano. Effective fault treatment for improving the dependability of cots and legacy-based applications. *IEEE Trans. Dependable Secur. Comput.*, 1(4):223–237, 2004. Member-Andrea Bondavalli.

[5] J. Gray. Why Do Computers Stop and What Can Be Done About It? *Proc. of Symposium on Reliability in Distributed Software and Database Systems*, 1986.

[6] David Oppenheimer and David A. Patterson. Studying and using failure data from large-scale internet services. In *EW10: Proceedings of the 10th workshop on ACM SIGOPS European workshop*, pages 255–258. ACM, 2002.

[7] Y. Huang, P. Jalote, and C. Kintala. Two Techniques for Transient Software Error Recovery. In *Workshop on Hardware and software architectures for fault tolerance: experiences and perspectives*, pages 159–170. Springer-Verlag, 1994.

[8] M. Sullivan and R. Chillarege. Software defects and their impact on system availability-a study of field failures in operating systems. *Fault-Tolerant Computing, 1991. FTCS-21. Digest of Papers., Twenty-First International Symposium*, pages 2–9, Jun 1991.

[9] J. Rosenthal R. Chillarege, S. Biyani. Measurement of Failure Rate in Widely Distributed Software. In *FTCS '95:Proc. of the Twenty-Fifth International Symposium on Fault-Tolerant Computing*, page 424. IEEE Computer Society, 1995.

[10] D. K. Pradham N. H.Vaidya. Safe System Level diagnosis. *IEEE Trans. on Computers*, 43(3):367–370, 1994.

[11] A. Pataricza J. Altmann, T. Bartha. On integrating error detection into a fault diagnosis algorithm for massively parallel computers. In *IPDS '95: Proceedings of the International Computer Performance and Dependability Symposium on Computer Performance and Dependability Symposium*, page 154, Washington, DC, USA, 1995. IEEE Computer Society.

[12] F.P. Preparata, G. Metze, and R.T. Chien. On the connection assignment problem of diagnosable systems. *Electronic Computers, IEEE Transactions on*, EC-16(6):848–854, Dec. 1967.

[13] Kaustubh R. Joshi, William H. Sanders, Matti A. Hiltunen, and Richard D. Schlichting. Automatic model-driven recovery in distributed systems. In *SRDS '05: Proceedings of the 24th IEEE Symposium on Reliable Distributed Systems*, pages 25–38. IEEE Computer Society, 2005.

[14] J.C. Laprie. Dependable Computing and Fault Tolerance: Concepts and Terminology. *Proc. of the 15th IEEE International Symposium on Fault-Tolerant Computing (FTCS-15)*, June 1985.

[15] Jean-Claude Laprie and Brian Randell. Basic concepts and taxonomy of dependable and secure computing. *IEEE Trans. Dependable Secur. Comput.*, 1(1):11–33, 2004. Fellow-Algirdas Avizienis and Senior Member-Carl Landwehr.

[16] D.P. Siewiorek R.S. Swarz. *Reliable Computer Systems (3rd ed.): Design and Evaluation.* A.K. Peters, 1998.

[17] Behrooz Parhami. From defects to failures: a view of dependable computing. *SIGARCH Comput. Archit. News*, 16(4):157–168, 1988.

[18] A. Avizienis and J. P. J. Kelly. Fault tolerance by design diversity: Concepts and experiments. *Computer*, 17(8):67–80, 1984.

[19] D. Avresky, J. Arlat, J. C. Laprie, and Y. Crouzet. Fault injection for formal testing of fault tolerance. *Reliability, IEEE Transactions on*, 45(3):443–455, 1996.

[20] M. Kalyanakrishnam R.K. Iyer, Z. Kalbarczyk. Measurement-Based Analysis of Networked System Availability. *Performance Evaluation Origins and Directions*, 2000.

[21] Bev Littlewood and Lorenzo Strigini. Software reliability and dependability: a roadmap. In *ICSE '00: Proceedings of the Conference on The Future of Software Engineering*, pages 175–188. ACM, 2000.

[22] J.K. Chaar et al. R. Chillarege, I.S. Bhandari. Orthogonal defect classification-a concept for in-process measurements. *IEEE Transactions on Software Engineering*, 18(11):943–956, 1992.

[23] Michael Grottke and Kishor S. Trivedi. Fighting bugs: Remove, retry, replicate, and rejuvenate. *Computer*, 40(2):107–109, 2007.

[24] Jeffrey A. Clark and Dhiraj K. Pradhan. Fault injection. *Computer*, 28(6):47–56, 1995.

[25] Kiran Nagaraja, Xiaoyan Li, Ricardo Bianchini, Richard P. Martin, and Thu D. Nguyen. Using fault injection and modeling to evaluate the performability of cluster-based services. In *USITS'03: Proceedings of the 4th conference on USENIX Symposium on Internet Technologies and Systems*, pages 2–2, Berkeley, CA, USA, 2003. USENIX Association.

[26] Y. Crouzet et al. J. Arlat, A. Costes. Fault injection and dependability evaluation of fault-tolerant systems. *IEEE Transactions on Computers*, 42(8):913–923, 1993.

[27] Joao Duraes and Henrique Madeira. Generic faultloads based on software faults for dependability benchmarking. In *DSN '04: Proceedings of the 2004 International Conference on Dependable Systems and Networks*, page 285. IEEE Computer Society, 2004.

[28] Jeffrey Voas, Gary McGraw, Lora Kassab, and Larry Voas. A 'crystal ball' for software liability. *Computer*, 30(6):29–36, 1997.

[29] M. Hiller Christmansson and M. Rimén. An experimental comparison of fault and error injection. In *ISSRE '98: Proceedings of the The Ninth International Symposium on Software Reliability Engineering*, page 369. IEEE Computer Society, 1998.

[30] Jeffrey Voas, Frank Charron, Gary McGraw, Keith Miller, and Michael Friedman. Predicting how badly "good" software can behave. *IEEE Softw.*, 14(4):73–83, 1997.

[31] Wee Teck Ng, C. M. Aycock, G. Rajamani, and P. M. Chen. Comparing disk and memory's resistance to operating system crashes. In *ISSRE '96: Proceedings of the The Seventh International Symposium on Software Reliability Engineering (ISSRE '96)*, page 182, Washington, DC, USA, 1996. IEEE Computer Society.

[32] J. Gabriel Silva J. Carreira, H. Madeira. Xception: A technique for the experimental evaluation of dependability in modern computers. *IEEE Trans. Software Engineering*, 24(2):125–136, 1998.

[33] Z. Segall, D. Vrsalovic, D. Siewiorek, D. Yaskin, J. Kownacki, J. Barton, R. Dancey, A. Robinson, and T. Lin. Fiat-fault injection based automated testing environment.

143

Fault-Tolerant Computing, 1988. FTCS-18, Digest of Papers., Eighteenth International Symposium on, pages 102–107, Jun 1988.

[34] Ghani A. Kanawati, Nasser A. Kanawati, and Jacob A. Abraham. Ferrari: A flexible software-based fault and error injection system. *IEEE Trans. Comput.*, 44(2):248–260, 1995.

[35] J. Christmansson and R. Chillarege. Generation of an Error Set that Emulates Software Faults Based on Field Data. In *Proc. of the The Twenty-Sixth Annual International Symposium on Fault-Tolerant Computing (FTCS '96)*, page 304. IEEE Computer Society, 1996.

[36] Henrique Madeira, Diamantino Costa, and Marco Vieira. On the emulation of software faults by software fault injection. In *DSN '00: Proceedings of the 2000 International Conference on Dependable Systems and Networks (formerly FTCS-30 and DCCA-8)*, pages 417–426. IEEE Computer Society, 2000.

[37] Arnaud Albinet, Jean Arlat, and Jean-Charles Fabre. Characterization of the impact of faulty drivers on the robustness of the linux kernel. In *DSN '04: Proceedings of the 2004 International Conference on Dependable Systems and Networks*, page 867. IEEE Computer Society, 2004.

[38] D. Tang W. Kao, R. K. Iyer. Fine: A fault injection and monitoring environment for tracing the unix system behavior under faults. *IEEE Trans. Softw. Eng.*, 19(11):1105–1118, 1993.

[39] H. Madeira et al. R. Moraes, J. Duraes. Injection of faults at component interfaces and inside the component code: are they equivalent? In *EDCC '06: Proceedings of the Sixth European Dependable Computing Conference*, pages 53–64. IEEE Computer Society, 2006.

[40] J. B. Dugan and K. S. Trivedi. Coverage modeling for dependability analysis of fault-tolerant systems. *IEEE Trans. Comput.*, 38(6):775–787, 1989.

[41] J. Christmansson and P. Santhanam. Error injection aimed at fault removal in fault tolerance mechanisms-criteria for error selection using field data on software faults. In *ISSRE '96: Proceedings of the The Seventh International Symposium on Software Reliability Engineering (ISSRE '96)*, page 175, Washington, DC, USA, 1996. IEEE Computer Society.

[42] J.-C. Fabre, F. Salles, M. Rodríguez Moreno, and J. Arlat. Assessment of cots microkernels by fault injection. In *DCCA '99: Proceedings of the conference on Dependable Computing for Critical Applications*, page 25, Washington, DC, USA, 1999. IEEE Computer Society.

[43] J. M. Bieman, D. Dreilinger, and Lijun Lin. Using fault injection to increase software test coverage. In *ISSRE '96: Proceedings of the The Seventh International Symposium on Software Reliability Engineering (ISSRE '96)*, page 166, Washington, DC, USA, 1996. IEEE Computer Society.

[44] Douglas M. Blough and Tatsuhiro Torii. Fault-injection-based testing of fault-tolerant algorithms in message-passing parallel computers. In *FTCS '97: Proceedings of the 27th International Symposium on Fault-Tolerant Computing (FTCS '97)*, page 258. IEEE Computer Society, 1997.

[45] Philip Koopman, John Sung, Christopher Dingman, Daniel Siewiorek, and Ted Marz. Comparing operating systems using robustness benchmarks. In *SRDS '97: Proceedings of the 16th Symposium on Reliable Distributed Systems (SRDS '97)*, page 72. IEEE Computer Society, 1997.

[46] D.P. Siewiorek et al. Development of a benchmark to measure system robustness. In *Digest of Papers FTCS-23 The Twenty-Third International Symposium on Fault-Tolerant Computing*, pages 88–97. IEEE Computer Society, 1993.

[47] Arup Mukherjee and Daniel P. Siewiorek. Measuring software dependability by robustness benchmarking. *IEEE Trans. Softw. Eng.*, 23(6):366–378, 1997.

[48] P. Koopman et al. The Ballista Robustness Testing Service. http://www.cs.cmu.edu/afs/cs.cmu.edu/project/edrcballista/www/index.html.

[49] N. P. Kropp, P. J. Koopman, and D. P. Siewiorek. Automated robustness testing of off-the-shelf software components. In *FTCS '98: Proceedings of the The Twenty-Eighth Annual International Symposium on Fault-Tolerant Computing*, page 230. IEEE Computer Society, 1998.

[50] Kobey Devale C.P. Shelton, P. Koopman. Robustness testing of the microsoft win32 api. In *2000 International Conference on Dependable Systems and Networks (DSN 2000) (formerly FTCS-30 and DCCA-8), 25-28 June 2000, New York, NY, USA*, pages 261–270, 2000.

[51] Karama Kanoun, Yves Crouzet, Ali Kalakech, Ana-Elena Rugina, and Philippe Rumeau. Benchmarking the Dependability of Windows and Linux using PostMark Workloads. In *16th International Symposium on Software Reliability Engineering (ISSRE 2005), 8-11 November 2005, Chicago, IL, USA*, pages 11–20, 2005.

[52] Ali Kalakech, Karama Kanoun, Yves Crouzet, and Jean Arlat. Benchmarking the dependability of windows NT4, 2000 and XP. In *2004 International Conference on Dependable Systems and Networks (DSN 2004), 28 June - 1 July 2004, Florence, Italy, Proceedings*, pages 681–686, 2004.

[53] Jean Arlat, Jean-Charles Fabre, Manuel Rodríguez, and Frédéric Salles. Dependability of cots microkernel-based systems. *IEEE Trans. Comput.*, 51(2):138–163, 2002.

[54] Diamantino Costa, Tiago Rilho, and Henrique Madeira. Joint evaluation of performance and robustness of a cots dbms through fault-injection. In *DSN '00: Proceedings of the 2000 International Conference on Dependable Systems and Networks (formerly FTCS-30 and DCCA-8)*, pages 251–260. IEEE Computer Society, 2000.

[55] Eric Marsden, Jean-Charles Fabre, and Jean Arlat. Dependability of CORBA systems: Service characterization by fault injection. In *Proceedings of the 21st Symposium on Reliable Distributed Systems (SRDS 2002), 13-16 October 2002, Osaka, Japan*, pages 276–285, 2002.

146

[56] Joseph Tucek, Shan Lu, Chengdu Huang, Spiros Xanthos, and Yuanyuan Zhou. Triage: diagnosing production run failures at the user's site. In *SOSP '07: Proceedings of twenty-first ACM SIGOPS symposium on Operating systems principles*, pages 131–144. ACM, 2007.

[57] Chun Yuan, Ni Lao, Ji-Rong Wen, Jiwei Li, Zheng Zhang, Yi-Min Wang, and Wei-Ying Ma. Automated known problem diagnosis with event traces. In *EuroSys '06: Proceedings of the 1st ACM SIGOPS/EuroSys European Conference on Computer Systems 2006*, pages 375–388, New York, NY, USA, 2006. ACM.

[58] Alice X. Zheng, Jim Lloyd, and Eric Brewer. Failure diagnosis using decision trees. In *ICAC '04: Proceedings of the First International Conference on Autonomic Computing*, pages 36–43. IEEE Computer Society, 2004.

[59] Yuriy Brun and Michael D. Ernst. Finding latent code errors via machine learning over program executions. In *ICSE '04: Proceedings of the 26th International Conference on Software Engineering*, pages 480–490. IEEE Computer Society, 2004.

[60] N. H. Vaidya and D. K. Pradham. Safe system level diagnosis. *IEEE Trans. Comput.*, 43(3):367–370, 1994.

[61] Andy Podgurski, David Leon, Patrick Francis, Wes Masri, Melinda Minch, Jiayang Sun, and Bin Wang. Automated support for classifying software failure reports. In *ICSE '03: Proceedings of the 25th International Conference on Software Engineering*, pages 465–475. IEEE Computer Society, 2003.

[62] Sunghun Kim, Jr. E. James Whitehead, and Yi Zhang. Classifying software changes: Clean or buggy? *IEEE Transactions on Software Engineering*, 34(2):181–196, March/April 2008.

[63] Marcos K. Aguilera, Jeffrey C. Mogul, Janet L. Wiener, Patrick Reynolds, and Athicha Muthitacharoen. Performance debugging for distributed systems of black boxes. In *SOSP '03: Proceedings of the nineteenth ACM symposium on Operating systems principles*, pages 74–89. ACM, 2003.

[64] Y.L.C. Chang, L.C. Lander, H.-S. Lu, and M.T. Wells. Bayesian analysis for fault location in homogeneous distributed systems. In *Reliable Distributed Systems, 1993. Proceedings., 12th Symposium on,* pages 44–53, Oct 1993.

[65] Gunjan Khanna, Ignacio Laguna, Fahad A. Arshad, and Saurabh Bagchi. Distributed diagnosis of failures in a three tier e-commerce system. In *SRDS '07: Proceedings of the 26th IEEE International Symposium on Reliable Distributed Systems,* pages 185–198, Washington, DC, USA, 2007. IEEE Computer Society.

[66] A. Brown, G. Kar, and A. Keller. An active approach to characterizing dynamic dependencies for problem determination in a distributed environment. In *In Seventh IFIP/IEEE International Symposium on Integrated Network Management,* 2001.

[67] Mike Y. Chen, Emre Kiciman, Eugene Fratkin, Armando Fox, and Eric Brewer. Pinpoint: Problem determination in large, dynamic internet services. In *DSN '02: Proceedings of the 2002 International Conference on Dependable Systems and Networks,* pages 595–604. IEEE Computer Society, 2002.

[68] Wei Chen, Sam Toueg, and Marcos Kawazoe Aguilera. On the quality of service of failure detectors. *IEEE Trans. Comput.,* 51(1):13–32, 2002.

[69] Jorrit N. Herder, Herbert Bos, Ben Gras, Philip Homburg, and Andrew S. Tanenbaum. Construction of a highly dependable operating system. In *EDCC '06: Proceedings of the Sixth European Dependable Computing Conference,* pages 3–12, Washington, DC, USA, 2006. IEEE Computer Society.

[70] IBM Press Release. Open, Secure, Scalable, Reliable, Unix for Power5 Servers, 2004.

[71] P.V. K. Iyer R.K. Iyer, L.T. Young. Automatic recognition of intermittent failures: An experimental study of field data. *IEEE Trans. Comput.,* 39(4):525–537, 1990.

[72] D.P. Siewiorek T.T.Y. Lin. Error Log analysis: Statistical Modeling and Heuristic Trend Analysis. *IEEE Transactions on Reliability,* 39(4):419–432, 1990.

[73] A. Thakur and B. K. Iyer. Analyze-now-an environment for collection and analysis of failures in a network of workstations. In *ISSRE '96: Proceedings of the The Seventh International Symposium on Software Reliability Engineering (ISSRE '96)*, page 14. IEEE Computer Society, 1996.

[74] Cristina Simache, Mohamed Kaâniche, and Ayda Saidane. Event log based dependability analysis of windows nt and 2k systems. In *PRDC '02: Proceedings of the 2002 Pacific Rim International Symposium on Dependable Computing*, page 311. IEEE Computer Society, 2002.

[75] Long Wang, Z. Kalbarczyk, Weining Gu, and R.K. Iyer. Reliability microkernel: Providing application-aware reliability in the os. *Reliability, IEEE Transactions on*, 56(4):597–614, Dec. 2007.

[76] Gunjan Khanna, Padma Varadharajan, and Saurabh Bagchi. Automated online monitoring of distributed applications through external monitors. *IEEE Trans. Dependable Secur. Comput.*, 3(2):115–129, 2006.

[77] Stephanie Forrest, Steven A. Hofmeyr, Anil Somayaji, and Thomas A. Longstaff. A sense of self for unix processes. In *SP '96: Proceedings of the 1996 IEEE Symposium on Security and Privacy*, page 120, Washington, DC, USA, 1996. IEEE Computer Society.

[78] S. H. Srinivasan R. P. Jagadeesh Chandra Bose. Data Mining Approaches to Software Fault Diagnosis. In *RIDE'05: Proc.of the 15th Workshop on Research Issues in Data Engineering: Stream Data Mining and Applications*, pages 45–52. IEEE Computer Society, 2005.

[79] Wenke Lee and Salvatore J. Stolfo. Data mining approaches for intrusion detection. In *SSYM'98: Proceedings of the 7th conference on USENIX Security Symposium*, pages 6–6. USENIX Association, 1998.

[80] Felix Salfner and Miroslaw Malek. Using hidden semi-markov models for effective online failure prediction. In *SRDS '07: Proceedings of the 26th IEEE International Symposium on Reliable Distributed Systems*, pages 161–174. IEEE Computer Society, 2007.

[81] M. F. Buckley and D. P. Siewiorek. VAX/VMS event monitoring and analysis. In *Proc. The 26th Annual Intl. Symp. on Fault-Tolerant Computing (FTCS '95)*, 1995.

[82] Cristina Simache and Mohamed Kaaniche. Availability assessment of sunos/solaris unix systems based on syslogd and wtmpx log files: A case study. In *PRDC '05: Proceedings of the 11th Pacific Rim International Symposium on Dependable Computing*, pages 49–56. IEEE Computer Society, 2005.

[83] Ram Chillarege. Self-testing software probe system for failure detection and diagnosis. In *Proc. of the 1994 conference of the Centre for Advanced Studies on Collaborative research*, page 10. IBM Press, 1994.

[84] Wu Linping, Meng Dan, Gao Wen, and Zhan Jianfeng. A proactive fault-detection mechanism in large-scale cluster systems. *Parallel and Distributed Processing Symposium, 2006. IPDPS 2006. 20th International*, pages 10 pp.–, April 2006.

[85] Christina Warrender, Stephanie Forrest, and Barak Pearlmutter. Detecting intrusions using system calls: Alternative data models. In *In IEEE Symposium on Security and Privacy*, pages 133–145. IEEE Computer Society, 1999.

[86] Alvaro A. Cárdenas, John S. Baras, and Karl Seamon. A framework for the evaluation of intrusion detection systems. In *SP '06: Proceedings of the 2006 IEEE Symposium on Security and Privacy*, pages 63–77. IEEE Computer Society, 2006.

[87] Larry M. Manevitz and Malik Yousef. One-class svms for document classification. *J. Mach. Learn. Res.*, 2:139–154, 2002.

[88] R. P. Jagadeesh Chandra Bose and S. H. Srinivasan. Data mining approaches to software fault diagnosis. In *RIDE '05: Proceedings of the 15th International Workshop on*

Research Issues in Data Engineering: Stream Data Mining and Applications, pages 45–52, Washington, DC, USA, 2005. IEEE Computer Society.

[89] Thorsten Joachims. *Text categorization with support vector machines: Learning with many relevant features.* Springer Verlag, 1998.

[90] Nathan Smith and Mark Gales. Speech recognition using svms. In *Advances in Neural Information Processing Systems 14*, pages 1197–1204. MIT Press, 2002.

[91] Zhonghui Hu, Yuangui Li, Yunze Cai, and Xiaoming Xu. Method of Combining Multi-class Svms Using Dempster-Shafer Theory and its Application. In *Proc. of American Control Conference (ACC'05)*. IEEE Computer Society, 2005.

[92] J. Shawe-Taylor N. Cristianini. *An Introduction to Support Vector Machines.* Cambridge University Press, 2000.

[93] Chih-Wei Hsu and Chih-Jen Lin. A comparison of methods for multiclass support vector machines. *Neural Networks, IEEE Transactions on*, 13(2):415–425, Mar 2002.

[94] John C. Platt and John C. Platt. Probabilistic outputs for support vector machines and comparisons to regularized likelihood methods. In *Advances in Large Margin Classifiers*, pages 61–74. MIT Press, 1999.

[95] A. Corsaro. CARDAMOM: A next generation mission and safety critical enterprise middleware. *Proc. of Workshop on Software Technologies for Future Embedded & Ubiquitous Systems*, pages 73–74, 2005.

[96] OMG. Fault tolerant corba standard, v2.5, 2001.

[97] Fabrizio Sebastiani. Machine learning in automated text categorization. *ACM Comput. Surv.*, 34(1):1–47, 2002.

[98] Regina L. O. Moraes, João Durães, R. Barbosa, Eliane Martins, and Henrique Madeira. Experimental risk assessment and comparison using software fault injection. In *Proc. of*

151

the 2007 International Conference on Dependable Systems and Networks (DSN'07), pages 512–521. IEEE Computer Society, 2007.